Tandy L Dix

The healthy infant, a treatise on the healthy procreation of the human race,

Embracing the obligations to offspring; the management of the pregnant female; the management of the newly born; the management of the infant; and the infant in sickness

Tandy L Dix

The healthy infant, a treatise on the healthy procreation of the human race,
Embracing the obligations to offspring; the management of the pregnant female; the management of the newly born; the management of the infant; and the infant in sickness

ISBN/EAN: 9783337728311

Printed in Europe, USA, Canada, Australia, Japan

Cover: Foto ©ninafisch / pixelio.de

More available books at **www.hansebooks.com**

The Healthy Infant,

A TREATISE ON THE

HEALTHY PROCREATION

—— OF ——

THE HUMAN RACE,

EMBRACING THE OBLIGATIONS TO OFFSPRING; THE MANAGEMENT OF THE PREGNANT FEMALE; THE MANAGEMENT OF THE NEWLY BORN; THE MANAGEMENT OF THE INFANT; AND THE INFANT IN SICKNESS.

By TANDY L. DIX, M. D.

Multum in Parvo.

CINCINNATI:
PETER G. THOMSON, PUBLISHER,
1880.

COPYRIGHT,
1879.
PETER G. THOMSON.

CONTENTS.

INTRODUCTORY.—Page 1.

PART I.—Page 5.

Obligations to Offspring—Showing the Duties we owe to Posterity, growing out of the Violations of the Moral Law, and the results to the Child.—The causes of City Children being unhealthy, and the healthfulness of Country Children.—Why City Children fail to recover their health when taken to the Country.—Of Licentiousness.—Of Law and Order; illustrated by the watch.—Of the Transmission of Parental Characteristics.—Of Inorganic and Organic Matter, and Cell Structure.—Of the Formation of the Primordial Cell.—Of the Spermatozoa.—Of the Organic and Animal Constructions of the Human Fabric.—The influence exerted by the Male and Female Parents upon the Offspring.—Of the Spiritual and Animal nature of Man; illustrated by the ass and the horse.—The cause of Hereditary Disease being more Transmissable from the Mother than from the Father.—The cause of Genius not descending from Father to Son.—Genius not a Factor in the Production of Genius.—Animal or Bodily Strength essential to the support and maintenance of a Great Mind.—The condition of the Mother that is essential to the production of a high order of Mind.—Reasons for cultivating the Organic rather than the Physical structure of the Female; and for cultivating the Physical Powers of the Male rather than his Organic Structure.—Of the Spiritual nature of Woman, and the Brutality of Man.—The Circumstances in which the highest Order of Minds most frequently appear.—The Growth of Beard, and other features which characterize the Male, are indicative of the blood pabulum for the production of the spermatozoa.—The effeminate features of the Female characterize the Blood Pabulum for the production of the Organic Body, the cell.—Of Female Education and Pursuits.—The Same of the Male.—Mixed Schools inimical to the Preparation of the Young for the part they are to perform in the Reproduction of the Race.—Of Early Marriage.

PART II.—Page 28.

Of the Fœtus in Utero.—Necessity of Protecting the Interests of the Fœtus.—Of the Relation which exists between the Mother and the Fœtus.—Of the Blood; its Conservative Power in maintaining a Healthy State.—Family Characteristics Transmitted through the Blood.—Hereditary Diseases.—Conditions of Matter, material and dynamic.—The Effects of Fear; illustrations of.—The Liability of the Fœtus to the Effects of Dynamic Forces, which affect it through the Organism of the Mother: (a) Alarm, dynamic force; (b) Normal changes in the Organism of the Mother; (c) Abnormal changes in the Organism of the Mother.—Of Mothers' Marks —Of the Siege of Landau; an interesting case, illustrating the effects of fright.—Of the Effects of Age.—The Importance of a Healthy State of both Parents at the time of Conception, and of the Mother during the entire term of uterine gestation.—Association.—Mental and Physical Exercise.—The food and dress of the Pregnant Woman.

PART III.—Page 58.

Management of the Newly-Born.—The manner in which the Newly-born is Treated, due to the State of Cultivation.—Of Birth.—Instinctive Desires and Reflex Action of the Nervous System.—The

Manner in which Christianized Society receives the Newly-born.—Of the Conditions most Compatible with its Organization.—Of the Senses.—Temperature.—The Care with which Animals and Birds protect their Young from Cold.—Necessity of Warmth Illustrated by the Attention of the Florist to the Temperature of his "Greenhouse."—Constitutions are to be Made.—The Conditions necessary to Breathing.—Deaths from Breathing Impure Air Arrested by the adoption of Dr. Clark's Suggestion to Ventilate the Buildings.—Of Inhalation, Exhalation, and the Circulation of the Blood.—Ablution of the Newly-born.—The Importance of the Mother nursing her own Babe.—The Manner in which the Infant should be put to the Breast.—Of *Colostrum.*—Of Colostration.—Food for the Young.—The Physiological Changes which transpire in the Mother during Uterine Gestation.—Of the Mecomium.—Of Yellow Milk; White Milk.—Of Sleep.

PART IV.—Page 80.

Infancy.—Of Infantile Organization.—The Discharge of Mucus.—Of the Muscular System.—Of Handling and Carrying the Infant.—Of Airing the Infant, and danger of Exposure.—Dentition; tooth formation. The Age at which the Several Teeth Appear.—Of Cutting the Gums.—Of Food for the Infant.—Of the Mother's Breast.—The Greatest Danger to the Infant Arising from Improper Feeding.—Precautionary Measures to be Taken in Feeding the Infant.—Improperly Prepared Food the Cause of the Death of Many Infants.—Liebig's Soup.—Carrot Pap.—Of Wet Nurses.—Of Clothing the Infant.—Of Weaning.

PART V.—Page 110.

The Infant in Sickness.—Selection and Preparation of the Sick Chamber.—Quietude.—Temperature.—Ventilation.—The Furniture,

Bedding and Medicines.—Sending for the Physician; His Reception; His Examination of the Patient.—Of the Company and Nurse.—Advice to the Mother in regard to her Neighbors; and to the Neighbors in regard to their Conduct toward the Sick.—How Visitors to the House of the Sick should be Received.—Of the Necessity of adhering strictly to the Directions of the Physician.—Administration of Medicines.—Of the Condition of the Eyes, Mouth and Nose.—Relief from the Suffering of Teething.—The Rescue of a Dying Infant by Cutting the Gums. Importance of Fresh Air to the Teething Infant.—The Importance of Early Detecting the illness of the Infant, and giving it Prompt Attention.

COLIC.—Page 131.

The Complaint with which the Infant is Most Frequently Afflicted.—Derivation of the word "Colic."—The Several Varieties of Colic.—Neuralgic, or Nervous Colic: Treatment.—Spasmodic, or Incidental Colic: Treatment.—Bilious Colic: Treatment.—Flatulency, or Wind Colic: Treatment —Inflammatory Colic: Treatment.—Colic Compounded of two or more of the Varieties: Treatment.

INTRODUCTORY.

In presenting a book to the public, the question naturally occurs: For what class or profession is the work designed? This question is usually answered by the title of the book. A treatise on disease is for the medical profession; on law, for the legal profession; and another on divinity, for theologians. Books are also written in the style, and with the technicalities peculiar to the science upon which they are written; and the reader is supposed to be so educated in that particular science as to be able to comprehend the full force and meaning of the terms used in illustration of the subject or science. Now, who shall be the reader of "The Healthy Infant?" To this we answer: EVERY ONE WHO FEELS ANY INTEREST AT ALL IN THE PROPAGATION OF THE RACE. Therefore, this work is addressed to both sexes; to the professional and unprofessional; and especially to the young—

for a healthy posterity will depend very much upon the degree of self-government which the latter exercise over their own actions, and also upon a knowledge of certain laws which pertain to reproduction, and which will enable them to secure to the offspring a freedom from many evils, which, with a reckless disregard of this knowledge, will bring misery and wretchedness to many succeeding generations. Hence, "THE HEALTHY INFANT" is written in plain and simple language, and free from all technicalities and obscurity of expression.

The author would respectfully call the attention of the reader to that portion of Part I. which treats of SEX, and the influence exerted upon the offspring by the male and female parents. He also hopes that he will not be considered as teaching the *doctrine of materialism*. The union of spirit and matter is only one of the innumerable phenomena that are beyond the comprehension of man. Although this union is so close that we cannot discover the dividing line between matter and spirit, yet there is sufficient evidence adduced in the following pages to show that there is a soul or mind or spirit, which is capable of exercising an influence over matter to such an extent as to cause the death of a local part— as was the case of the man with stone in the bladder; and on the other hand, we know that the condition of matter exercises a marked influence upon the soul or mind or spirit of the man; for when his liver is torpid, or the bowels constipated, he has the—*blues*, which occasionally result in suicide. We further know that the soul or mind or spirit is especially associated with the vital organs, and not with the animal or mechanical construction of the fabric, as are the extremities; for these may be wanting, and yet "*the soul liveth.*" Therefore, as the father supplies, *mainly*, the mechanical or animal construction to the offspring, and the mother the organic construction, the type of the former is discovered in the general make-up of the body, and the type of the latter in the talents and dispositions of the minds of the offspring.

Those who are contemplating a change from a single to a married state, owe it to posterity, in selecting their companions, to keep the interests of posterity in view, rather than prostitute to their personal aggrandizement that sacred marital law which was handed from the portals of heaven directly to man. This law marks the identity of families, communities, states, and Nations. It secures to the heir, his patrimony; to the prince, his crown. Yet, still more important, and in accordance with its design, is the propagation of the race. Therefore, those who enter into this relation incur the obligation of protecting every interest of posterity.

THE
HEALTHY INFANT.

PART I.

ON PARENTAL OBLIGATIONS TO OFFSPRING.

In looking abroad upon the varied conditions of our race, we find in many of our fellow-beings evidences of mental and physical incapacity. We find many instances of those who perish from diseases, transmitted from generation to generation; and of those diseases we have sad reminders in our midst, in the shape of Asylums, Almshouses, Institutes for Feeble-Minded, and Charity Hospitals. Notwithstanding the number who suffer from debility, and the lives sacrificed by hereditary disease, mankind seems not to be satisfied; but each successive generation magnifies the evils it inherited by adding its proportion of those which arise from human depravity. Against this depravity, civilized society protects itself by the criminal law, prison houses, and the gallows. In view of all this, the question naturally arises, Whence cometh all these evils? And the usual response is: "From Eve, the prime mother of us all."

Thus generation after generation has endeavored to shift the burden from its conscience, to the first child-bearer; and so avoid responsibility for its own willful and egregious sins. When the tempter prevailed on her to eat the forbidden fruit, she did not stop to look down the current of human events and behold the untold evils she might be bestowing upon innocent posterity. She knew nothing of her progeny, and certainly little, if anything, of what she was entailing upon them. Her mind was entirely engaged in the pleasantness of the fruit to her taste, and its boasted power of making herself and consort "as Gods, knowing good and evil." Now, the present generation enjoys this knowledge, combined with the experience of thousands of years as to the terrible results accruing to posterity from our own actions; yet many daughters of Eve blindly rush into marriage without a thought of the misery they may be preparing for their posterity—oblivious of everything but their own selfish gratification; and thinking they are nobody's "keepers" but their own. Thus the stream of human life, polluted by the fall at its source, increases in impurity as it flows on. It becomes more and more defiled by individual folly and crime; and its corrupted and poisonous qualities are seen in shortened human lives, in which more sin and misery are crowded than was found in the far longer earthly pilgrimages of the patriarchs.

It is upon parents and guardians that the obligations rest of implanting those principles in the young, and endowing them with that extent of knowledge which will qualify them for thinking and acting intelligently, wisely, and purely in the matter of the propagation of the species, so that the stream of life shall become, comparatively at least, pure;

human suffering be kept within due bounds, and the duration of life be limited only by natural causes. By this means a high degree of perfection of character and consequent happiness will be secured to our race ; for the mitigation of our bodily ailments upon which so large a share of that happiness depends, is only to be realized by the correction of our mental and moral deficiencies.

It is manifest that equally with the physical conformation of the parents, their progeny also inherits their moral bias, mental deficiencies, and bodily ailments. Hence, parents seem to continue their lives in their descendants. Like the Claudian family, which through many generations exhibited a continuous and even inflamed malignity of disposition until it reached the utmost height of its revolting intensity in Nero, "the tyrant, the scourge of mankind, and the incendiary of Rome." Thus posterity carries with it the virtues and the vices, the health and diseases, of its ancestry. This is the source of the greater part of the evils which come under the observation of the moralist and of the physician, who are often charged with inefficiency in correcting moral bias and bodily ailments, notwithstanding the increased diffusion of knowledge, and the advancements in the medical sciences afford increased facilities for so doing. Thus being held, in some degree, responsible for the impurities of the stream of human life, it then becomes our bounden duty to learn as much as we can of the history of our ancestry, that we may cultivate our inherited virtues and avoid our inherited vices. We must connect with this a knowledge of organic law, and of the natural laws of health. This will enable us to guard against inherited tendencies to particular diseases; and will also teach us the importance of avoiding those pernicious influences and habits which depress the vital forces, impair the integrity of organic life, and thus invite the development of latent hereditary affections which otherwise would have become extinct. Even in the absence of hereditary tendencies, the disorders of the constitution, effected by irregular habits and pernicious indulgences, will be transmitted to the offspring. The child upon whom is entailed an unhappy existence may truly point back to his forefathers as the progenitors of his afflictions as well as of his being. The causes which produce so much suffering and loss of life are clearly attributable to the many dissipations, excesses, abuses of the animal economy, evil associations, and such amusements as lower the natural and healthy tone of the mind. The laws of health are dependent upon the delicate and intricate connection subsisting between the various organs, the exactness of their functions, and their free and unrestrained exercise. When, therefore, these laws are interfered with and encroached upon, and even positively violated by late hours, frequent parties, abnormal indulgence of the appetite, the midnight dance, and the opera—the human system is radically undermined and rendered utterly unfit for increasing and multiplying its kind. Those day and night draughts upon the vital forces entirely break up the beautiful machine of the human body, and leave the immortal soul a mere empty bag of wind, suited to no good use whatever.* The result to the offspring is a patrimony of debility. As a panacea, the

---

*The principal sources of degeneracy which appear at present to be most active in their influence for evil on large masses of mankind may be stated as follows: (1.) Degeneracy from Toxæmia, or from the abuse of alcoholic fluids, opium, preparations of Indian hemp (hashish), tobacco, and the like; also, from

anxious parent sends his child to the rural districts, where the parents live more in accordance with natural law, and the result to the offspring is vigorous health. The prime cause of the healthfulness of country children is lost sight of by the city parents, who fail to discover in their own bad habits the prolific source of the infirmities of their children; and while these habits are demanded by the follies of social life, it is to be regretted that frail humanity yet further descends into the lowest revelries of licentiousness, and brings from thence the seeds of still greater evils to posterity. Although the married state ought to remove the temptation to the indulgence of licentious habits, yet these are to be found among married people; and the offspring is more apt to suffer, as there is not sufficient time before the act of reproduction to admit of the parents recovering from the effects of such indulgence. And surely it is not expected to ob-

---

the effects of lead, mercury, arsenic, phosphorus; and from the use of unwholesome vegetable food, such as diseased rye, maize, wheat, and the like. (2.) Degeneracy from the persistent and pernicious influence of malaria. (3) Degeneracy from certain peculiar geological formations, soil and water, as in the development of goitre. (MACLELLAN, WATSON.) See paper on Hygiene of India, in *Med. Chir. Review.* (4.) Degeneracy from the effects of epidemic diseases which now and then afflict large populations, profoundly influencing the system, and engendering those morbid temperaments whose types are fully expressed in the generations which follow the one that has suffered from such epidemic pestilences. Many of such like epidemics act like toxic agents on the nervous system. (5.) Degeneracy from the effects of the "*great town system*," as the phrase is. The chief elements of such degeneracy are: (*a*) Unhealthy situations; (*b.*) a noxious local and general atmosphere; (*c.*) insufficient atmosphere; (*d.*) insufficient and improper nourishment; (*e.*) deleterious avocations; (*f.*) moral and social misery, wretchedness, and crime. (6.) Degeneracy from fundamental morbid states, congenital or acquired, as seen in imperfect cerebral developments, deaf mutism, blindness, constitutional diseases, and diathesis (implanted, hereditary, or acquired), such as syphilis and scrofulosis. (7.) Degeneracy from mixed causes, from marrying in and in, and from other causes not included in the above. (*Med. Chir. Review,* Jan., 1858: AITKEN, "Science of Practice.")

tain good fruit from bad trees; or a plentiful harvest from impoverished or uncultivated lands. Those who raise cattle and horses pay strict attention to the stock, that it may be of the best and most productive kind. In so doing they act upon a recognized principle that to have good progeny, the progenitors must likewise be good. The material interest of man makes him appreciate the importance of having a knowledge of the laws of healthy production and development in the animal and vegetable kingdoms. But the evils resulting from the gratification of our own desires are not always immediate; they are often removed from our sight to appear in future generations, the representatives of which will perhaps be taught, not to regard their ancestors as at all responsible, but to consider their afflictions as either providential visitations, in consequence of their own transgressions of the moral law, or as the results of their own violations of the laws of health. For these reasons, married people, more especially, should guard against excessive indulgence and violations of the laws of health, and correct morals, but more particularly against the baneful, contaminating and demoralizing effects of adultery. The penalties of this sin often fall heavily upon posterity, constituting for it, indeed, a wretched inheritance.

From the foregoing we may conclude that we are created to live by law, and to be subject to order, and not made over to the uncertainties of chance. In fact, the elementary constituents of inorganic compounds, no less than organized bodies, the phenomena of reproduction, and the continuance of life are in accordance with law. Now, were it possible to keep these laws inviolate, and the Great Lawmaker not arrest their exercise, organized matter would continue through interminable ages, for all we know. In order that the human organization may continue in the performance of its functions uninterruptedly, it is therefore necessary that these laws should be studied and understood, and the importance of complying with their demands be appreciated. When we look upon the face of a watch and see the hands pointing at figure after figure, our admiration is excited by the regularity and the exactitude of their movements. But on opening it, we discover how delicate is the machinery that is necessary to satisfy the laws of nature; and how slight a derangement of apparently a very insignificant part will disarrange the whole mechanism. When it came from the hands of its maker it had all of its part complete. It was made of durable substances—brass and gold. Its movements will continue until it is worn out or broken. It requires no attached apparatus to prepare material for its daily sustenance. Its object is single — the keeping of time. Hence there is no necessity for a combination of systems or organs.

When we keep in mind the absolute necessity of a strict compliance with law in the construction of, comparatively, so simple a mechanical apparatus as a watch, we shall better appreciate the existence of a much higher order of laws when we come to study that more admired and beautiful structure—the human economy. Although much of the beauty and excellency of these laws, by their intricacy and obscurity, escapes our understanding, yet there are many phenomena which will, by proper interpretation, be our guides for apprehending them in some degree.

How different from the watch is man! The imperfections acquired from parents are usually irreparable. They will, most likely, be transmitted to each succeeding child. He does not come into the world complete; but, to be developed. His proximate component parts are not elementary substances, but gases, combined according to their laws of affinity. When he is resolved into his ultimate chemical constituents, there remains only a few ounces of earthy matter. He is not at once supplied with the requisite quantity of material for his existence and movements, but is furnished with an apparatus for the elaboration of material for the construction of his body, and for the removal of waste matters. The object of his being is not single, but manifold. Hence the necessity for organs and systems of organs. Their connections are specially delicate, and the disturbance of one comparatively insignificant part is promptly reflected to other parts, and is productive of a greater variety of derangements than would occur with the watch. Deficiencies in the watch may be supplied, and imperfectly arranged parts may be re-adjusted; but in man it is sadly the reverse, as his deficiencies and derangements are not only irreparable, but transmissible through many generations. A due consideration of the foregoing ought to induce a high appreciation of a knowledge of the laws of health and of reproduction, and the importance of complying with all the demands which they impose upon us as a duty to posterity.

As we may reasonably conclude that the offspring partakes of the nature of the parent in its psychical and physical constitutions, it now remains to consider those laws which govern the transmission of parental characteristics.

The attention of the reader has already been called to the classification of matter under two general heads, viz: *inorganic* and *organic*. The former is represented by the mineral, and the latter by the animal and vegetable kingdom. The distinguishing feature of the latter class, or organic matter, is the cell structure. A cell may be described as a bubble, so small as to be seen and studied only under the microscope. When many of these are united they form tissue, of which animal and vegetable matters are composed; therefore, all organic bodies, whether man or insect, trees or plants, consist of a congeries of cells. This structure is beautifully displayed in the leaf of a flower when highly magnified. From a single cell, called the primordial or parent cell, or germ produced by the parent—a type of which is found in the "tread" of the hen's egg—proceed all the succeeding cells, called daughter cells, by duplication. Thus the parent cell produces two; each of these two produce two others, and so continue multiplying by twos until a body is formed like the parent which gave origin to the primordial cell. A remarkable feature of the parent cell is, that those of the several races of animals, and those of the vegetable kingdom, are so similar in appearance as to make it impossible to determine, upon examination, whether it would germinate into a human being, an animal, a fish, a fowl, a tree, or a plant. Yet, notwithstanding its minuteness and indistinctness of character, it seems to possess the power of determining the shape and size of the offspring, the character of its organic structure, and the manner in which the organs shall perform their vital functions. These are certainly great issues to proceed from a body so small.

From the foregoing we can fully appreciate the importance of the cell in the production of the offspring, and are forced to the conclusion that the cell is endowed with some attribute peculiar to itself, independent of the impregnating fluid of the male. This conclusion is still farther strengthened when we contrast the male secretion with the female cell. The latter is an *organized body, in miniature;* and is not, *as a cell*, secreted from the blood of the mother. There is a small bladder, the "*graafian vesicle*," or "*ovisac*" in the stroma of the ovary, a small organ situated one on each side of the womb, within which the parent cell is *formed* and *organized* out of material supplied by the blood of the mother, and through the lining membrane of the ovisac. The parent cell is thus organized under the direct influence of the life-giving power of the blood of the mother; and is thereby impressed with a type of her organism; and this type passes into the organic structure of the offspring. *It is for this reason that the influence of the female supersedes the male parent in the formation of the brain, and of the organs within the trunk.*

The cell, as supplied by the mother, is of short duration, but when it is impregnated with the male fluid, it starts on its course in the formation of the fœtus. This fluid possesses no cell structure, although it contains the spermatozoa, which are very active in their movements. This activity proceeds from their animal nature, as the name implies, being derived from the two Greek words: *sperma* (seed), and *zoōn* (an animal). Their function in reproduction is to supply the animal construction to the offspring. Therefore, the *influence of the male supersedes that of the female parent in the animal construction of the organism.*

We have just seen that matter is divisible into *inorganic* and *organic* bodies;* that the CELL is the distinguishing fea-

---
*The cell is a *sine qua non* to the existence of an organized body; but not to organic matter—as the white of an egg, or the spermatozoa are organic matters, but are not organic organized bodies.

ture of the latter, and that organic bodies consist of a congeries of cells. We will now confine our remarks to the animal creation, including man, and will consider the subject under two heads, viz: the animal, and the organism or organical construction of the animal. By the animal construction is meant the framework which gives support and strength to the body; and consists in the *bone, muscle, fibroid, and cellular tissue,* which *enter into the construction of every organ* and portion of the body. The organism, or organical construction, pertains to the vital organs, the brain, and the organs contained in the trunk. The vital organs give rise to, and determine the greatness and the qualities of the spirit or soul of the being. The ass and the horse supply a marked illustration of the different degrees and qualities of the mind, or spirit, or soul* that can be produced by vital organs. The former is preëminently an animal, and shows his brutal nature in every feature, notwithstanding his vital organs are anatomically like those of the horse, which possesses such organs as will supply a spirit that animates and raises him far above the asinine creature. Now, the female parent supplies an organized body *in miniature—the* CELL, which determines the organical construction of the vital organs; the manner in which these are to perform their functions; and, consequently, the extent and qualities of the spirit, or soul, or mind of the offspring.

There are phenomena of daily occurrence in the productions of the animal creation which can not be explained upon any hypothesis other than the one given above. First among these prominently stands the fact that hereditary

---

*All animals possess, in some degree, a spirit, or soul, or mind; but none, *except man*, are endowed with immortality.

diseases of the vital organs are more apt to be transmitted from the mother to the offspring than from the father. We also find here sufficient explanation of the child inheriting the general features and make-up of the father; whereas the general disposition of the mind, and the manner in which the vital organs perform their functions, are strongly marked by those which characterize the mother. And still farther, Dr. Carpenter, in his "Principles of Physiology," says: "It has long been a prevalent idea, that certain parts of the organism* of the offspring are derived from the male, and certain other parts from the female parent; and although no universal rule can be laid down upon this point, yet the independent observations which have been made by numerous practical 'breeders' of domestic animals (both mammals and birds) seem to establish that such a *tendency* has a real existence, the characters of the *animal* portion of the organism being especially, (but not exclusively) derived from the *male* parent, and those of the *organic* apparatus being in like manner derived from the *female* parent. The former will be chiefly manifested in the external appearance, in the general configuration of the head and limbs, in the organs of the senses (including the skin), and in the locomotive apparatus; whilst the latter show themselves in the size of the body (which is primarily determined by the development of the viscera contained in the trunk) and in the mode in which the vital functions are performed. Thus the *mule*, which is the produce of the male ass and the mare, is essentially a *modified ass*, having the general configuration of its sire (slightly varied by equine peculiarities), but having the rounder trunk and the larger size of its dam; on the

---

*Here "*organism*" means the whole body, including the extremities.

other hand, the *hinny*, which is the offspring of the stallion and the she-ass, is essentially a *modified horse*, having the general configuration of the horse (though with a slight admixture of asinine features), but being a much smaller animal than its sire, and thus approaching its dam in size, as well as in the comparative narrowness of its trunk." Here we have an illustration of the influence which the male and the female parents *separately* exert in the production of the offspring that is clear to the understanding, full in the details, and complete in all of its parts.

Now, in the application of these principles to the reproductions of the human race, we will take, as the basis of our remarks, the following quotation from a most excellent work on infancy, by Dr. A. Combe, who says:

"It is a very common saying, that clever men have generally stupid children, and that those of men of genius are little better than fools: and the inference is drawn, that the constitution of the father has very little influence on that of the children. I admit the fact that the families of men of genius are rarely remarkable for talent: but deduce from it a directly opposite conclusion, and maintain that those very cases are proof of the reality of the father's influence on the constitution of his descendants, and consequently direct warnings for our guidance. If we consider for a moment the state of health and general mode of life of men of genius, what can be farther removed from the standard of nature? Are they not, as a race, enthusiastic, excitable, irregular, the sport of every passing emotion, and, almost without exception, martyrs to indigestion, and often to melancholy? And are these the seeds from which nature has designed *healthy* vigor of mind and body to spring up in their offspring? Take into account, also, the influence of the mother, and the well-known fact that men of genius rarely select the highly-gifted in the opposite sex for their partners through life, and then say whether high talent can reasonably be expected to emanate from parents, one of whom, the mother, rises at best only to mediocrity, and the other, the father, falls temporarily, to or below it, from sheer exhaustion of mind and broken health. Would it not rather be wonderful, if, in such untoward circumstances, the genius were to descend in unabated splendor, even to the first line of the posterity? It is not from such materials that living genius has sprung, and never will be; for even were the child to inherit all the father's fire, he would receive along with it a morbid delicacy and irritability of temperament, which would render it impossible for him to survive the period of early infancy. A genius might, in some favorable moment, be *born* to such a father; but he would die before the world could tell that a genius had lived. The circumstances in which the highest order of minds most frequently appear, are where the father is healthy and active, and the mother unites an energetic character with vigorous bodily health, or with some high-sustaining excitement animating all her mental and bodily functions. The mother of Bonaparte was of this description; and the mothers of most of our celebrated men will be found to have been more or less distinguished for similar characteristics; and, accordingly, how often in the biographies of men of genius do we remark that it was the mother who first perceived and fanned the flame which burst into after brightness! Taking the whole circumstances, then, into consideration, the influence of the father, although often less strong than that of the mother, remains unquestionable, and the exception in the case of men of genius is not real, but only apparent from being imperfectly understood."

This is certainly strong argument. But is it true? Does it accord with physiological fact? Does it tell us what constitutes sex? Does it give a satisfactory explanation of genius not descending from father to son? In remarking upon this quotation, it may be observed, first, that the cause of genius, not descending from father to son, is ascribed to "*the state of health and mode of life of men of genius.*" The fallacy of the notion that genius is hereditary becomes apparent when we consider the fact that the fathers of men of genius are usually *ordinary* and *obscure men;* and as genius rarely ever descends from father to son, we may justly conclude that this order of mind is not a factor in the production of men of genius. Again, the non-hereditary character of genius is evident from the fact that when nature directs her efforts in the construction of a brain of great powers, she does so at the expense of the animal powers of the structure. This obtains among children who are unduly pressed in their studies, whose brain expansion is at the expense of their physical development. For this reason, also, men of genius have not the ability to resist excessive indulgences; if animal power does not respond to their will in their own natures, they seek for some external substitute, which answers their purpose so long as it lasts, but when the stimulus vanishes, they find themselves in the depths of gloom and despair. Now, the nature of a father so artificially excited cannot supply the CELL with such a degree of animal strength as will support so great an amount of brain force; *for even were the child to inherit all the father's fire, he would, for want of a proper* ANIMAL CONSTRUCTION, *receive along with it a morbid delicacy, and irritability of temperament, which would render it impossible for him to survive the period of early infancy.*" Attention may be called to the fact that our author has not mentioned *genius* among the "circumstances in which the highest order of minds most frequently appear." But "*where the father is* HEALTHY *and* ACTIVE," NOT *where he is a* GENIUS, do we find HEALTHY *and* ACTIVE *spermatozoa*, from which spring the animal parts of the structure capable of *supporting* the "highest order of minds." Among the "circumstances" pertaining to the mother, no mention is made of the "highly-gifted of the opposite sex," because this also is not found, practically, to be a factor in the production of men of genius. The course of reasoning our author pursues indicates that he arrived at his conclusions expressed in the "circumstances" by observing the results obtained from the various conditions under which our race is constantly being reproduced, instead of having drawn them from physiological research. This sufficiently explains the seeming discrepancy between his course of reasoning and his conclusions. When the practical results as obtained from the reproductions of the race are brought into view side by side with the line of argument presented here in support of the teachings of physiology, we find them to harmonize in a most beautiful and striking manner. It is quite pertinent to inquire why the "*highly-gifted* in the opposite sex" is not a factor in the production of superior minds? This finds a solution: first, in the fact that a mother can possess this order of mind without either an energetic character or bodily health; second, she may possess all these, and yet lack that very essential one, "high and sustaining excitement animating all her mental and bodily functions." For it is this animated state that *deeply impresses* the cell with *organical constructive power and brain force.* To whatever degree the former may exist, without this latter circumstance genius can NEVER be transmitted to the offspring. Our author proceeds to show the truthfulness of these circumstances by referring to the character of the mothers who produce most of our great men—"first perceived and fanned the flame which burst into after brightness." He concludes thus:

"Taking the whole circumstance into consideration, the influence of the father, although often less strong than that of the mother, remains unquestionable, and the exception in the case of men of genius is not real, but only apparent from being imperfectly understood."

Hence it is seen that a *perfect* knowledge of *"the whole circumstances"* shows that physiology does not demand *any* of the brilliant qualities of the father for the adornment of the son; but only *requires* the full *strength of his animal powers* to give *support* and *strength* to the *physical development of the offspring.* Therefore, the case of men of genius forms *no exception* to the laws of reproduction, but goes *far* to show the direction in which nature designs the influence of the *male parent* to be *exerted in the production of the offspring.*

From the physiology of the production of the *parent cell*—its organic construction passing into the vital organs of the offspring; and, determining the manner in which these organs shall perform their functions—we learn the importance of cultivating the *organic*, rather than the *physical or animal*, construction of the female. Whereas, the physiology of the spermatozoa, their animal construction passing into the physical structures of the organism, does teach the importance of cultivating the animal, rather than the organic construction of the male. As nature is ever true to herself, she has assigned the charge of the offspring and the household affairs to the female as her special duties in life, as studies, literature, verse, music, drawing, and painting, are peculiarly adapted to her nature. This cultivation of the organic construction of the female enables her to endure the annoyances and confinement which those duties impose upon her; while by nature man is peculiarly adapted to the plow-handle, the work-shop, the legislative hall, and the battle-field—these strengthen his animal powers, and dull the sensitiveness of his organism, whereby he is enabled to endure the hardships to which he is exposed.*

---

*"Horum omnium fortissimi sunt Belgæ, propterea quod a cultu atque humanitate provinciæ longissime absunt, minimeque ad eos mercatores sæpe commeant, *atque ea quæ ad effeminandos animos* pestinent *important.*"

From the foregoing, we discover sex, in the female, to consist in the predominance of the organic over the animal part of the structure, and is manifested in the skin being softer, the hair finer, and the bones and muscles smaller than in the male; and in the lack of beard; and additional sets of organs—the uterus and mammary glands. She is characterized by softness, sensibility, and modesty; whereas, the predominance of the animal in man, is characterized by boldness, firmness, and muscular strength :

"Women are soft, mild, pitiful, and flexible;
Thou, stern, obdurate, flinty, rough, remorseless."

The softness and mildness of the female is due to her nearer approach to the spiritual state in which we will exist when the soul is separated from the body, "*where flesh and blood cannot enter.*" ANGELS, therefore, differ from women in their freedom from the contaminations of the flesh; and as woman has less of the *animal* in the *construction* of her organism, she is therefore PURER; and, in her *fall*, she *descends* from a *higher* state of *purity* than *man*, and *descends* to a *lower depth* of *degradation*—with the chances of her *reformation* far more *precarious*.

We have already considered the necessity of complying with law to obtain true happiness and substantial success; and have seen that when irregularities are substituted for law, evil results will ensue; and in the affairs of men, there is no law, the violation of which will bring greater evils upon our race than those which pertain to the sexes. Whenever one of the fairer sex claims to be one of the "stronger minded," and endeavors to cope with man, she relinquishes her claim upon his protective care; and will, by becoming masculine, cease to be the object of his love and admiration.* On the other hand, we find that the male, by constantly performing the duties peculiar to female life, will become so effeminate as to lose the admiration of the opposite sex :

> "A woman, impudent and mannish grown,
> Is not more loathed, than an effeminate man
> In time of action."

Those are *not* the circumstances in which the highest order of minds most frequently appear, but are perversions of the law established by DEITY, from which *great evils accrue* to posterity in the shape of effeminate men with feeble minds. Now, let the effeminate man and the masculine woman be contrasted with the requirements of natural law as set forth in the following quotation, and see if such should be selected for the propagation of a healthy and vigorous race. Dr. Carpenter, in his Principles of Physiology, says:

" But, farther, there are many examples in which the presence of a certain substance in the blood appears to determine the formation of the particular tissue, of which that substance is the appropriate pabulum.† And thus as the abstraction of the material required for each part leaves the blood in a state fitted for the nutrition of other parts, it seems to follow, as Mr. Paget has further remarked, that such a mutual dependence exists amongst the several parts and organs of the body as causes the evolution of one to supply the conditions requisite for the production of another; and hence, that the order in which the several organs of the body appear in the course of devel-

---

*The masculine or animal nature of some men is so great as to lower the man, almost, to the level of the brute. Esau was somewhat of this character—all over, like a hairy garment, . . . and was a cunning hunter." Such a man was not permitted to receive the blessings of so good a man as Isaac; and to be a patriarch in the house of Israel.

†In the blood of the female is the appropriate pabulum for the formation of the cell; and in the blood of the male is the appropriate pabulum for the construction of the spermatozoon.

opment, while it is conformable to the law of imitation of the parent, and to the law of progressive ascent towards the higher grade of beings, is yet the immediate result of changes effected in the conditions of the blood by the antecedent operations. And this view is confirmed by many circumstances, which indicate that certain organs really do stand in such a *complemental* relation to one another as it implies; a large class of facts of this order being supplied by the history of the evolution of the generative apparatus, and by that of concurrent changes in other organs (especially in the integumentary) which are found to be dependent upon it, although there is no direct functional relation between them.

"Thus the growth of beard in man, at the period of puberty, is but a type of a much more important change which takes place in many animals with every recurrence of the period of generative activity. This is most obvious in birds, whose plumage, at the commencement of the breeding season, becomes (especially in the male) more highly colored, besides being augmented by the growth of new feathers; but when the sexual organs pass into their state of periodic atrophy, the plumage at once begins to assume a paler and more sombre hue, and many of the feathers are usually cast, their nutrition being no longer kept up.

"It is a matter of common observation, that the deficiency of hair on the face (where this is not, as among the Asiatics, a characteristic of race) is usually concurrent with a low amount of generative power in the male, and may be considered as indicative of it; whilst, on the other hand, the presence of hair on the upper-lip and chin of the female, is indicative of a tendency in the general organization and mental character towards the attributes of the male, and of a deficiency in those which are typical of the female.

"If, moreover, the development of the male organs be prevented, the evolution of the beard does not take place; whilst the strong growth of hair on the face, as well as by other changes, may be attributed to the presence of some special nutritive material in the blood, for which there is no longer any other demand. This again shows itself yet more strongly in birds, among which (as Hunter long since pointed out) it is no uncommon occurrence for the female, after ceasing to lay, to assume the plumage of the male, and even to acquire other characteristic parts, as the spurs in the fowl tribe. Moreover, it has been ascertained by the experience of Sir Philip Egerton, that if a buck be castrated while his antlers are growing and are still covered with the velvet, their growth is checked, they remain as if truncated, and irregular nodules of bone project from their surfaces; whilst if the castration be performed when the antlers are full grown, they are shed nearly as usual at the end of the season, but in the next season are only replaced by a kind of low, conical stumps."

From what we have already seen, and in connection with this quotation, it is very clear, indeed, that the female, by following the pursuits which naturally belong to the male, will cultivate that principle, or pabulum, which is formed in the blood for the reproduction of the race—for the *production* of *spermatozoa*, rather than for the *formation* of the *organic body, the cell*. In proportion to the extent of this cultivation, so will be the external masculine appearance of the female, and less vigorous will be the ORGANIC CONSTRUCTION of the *cell;* and, therefore, her offspring will be deficient in mind, spirit, or soul. These same principles apply with equal force to the male. Effeminating influences will effeminate his spermatozoa, and his offspring will be deficient in *stamina.*

Another obligation to the succeeding generation arising out of what constitutes *sex* is, the method of training the female mind. The course of study best adapted to her nature, and which will more fully prepare her for the part she is destined to perform in the reproduction of the race, is one that will stimulate the mental faculties, and enliven the vital organs in the performance of their functions; and to such an extent as will develop the reasoning powers, and yet not depress the organism. By such a course of study, with indulgence only in those refinements and habits natural to the sex, she will make true advances to the standard of her nature, and heighten the purity, strength, and nobility of her character, and will, in a great measure, supply a "*high and sustaining excitement, animating all her mental and bodily functions.*"

The male mind, on the contrary, should be trained in the deeper researches of the languages, arts, and sciences—these bringing out the animal or masculine strength of the brain, and enabling him to cope with the widest sphere of intelligence; man with man, and nation with nation. It is thus man is enabled to obtain the advantages which are derived from mechanics, art, science, religion, peace, politics, and war—wherein are found the problems with which the mental powers of man must grapple, and are beyond the effeminate powers of the female mind.

It is, then, quite obvious that "*mixed*" institutions of learning cannot supply the mental training best adapted to either of the sexes, as both must pursue the same course of studies. This method of education will cause the one to assimilate the characteristics of the other—the female will become masculine, and the male effeminate. And what else can, finally, be expected, but a race degenerate in mind and body—imbecile? Therefore, let our daughters become *women*, and our sons become *men*. These ends can be obtained by sending our daughters to female schools, where they are daily associated with things and studies which tend to effeminate the *blood*, and, consequently, the mind and body; and our sons to male schools, where the studies, and the things with which they are associated, will make their *blood* masculine. This method of education will produce women and men, who are such in the *full* and *expressed* language of nature's God; will greatly intensify the pleasures which arise from the mingling of the sexes in the social and family circles, and greatly contribute to supplying the "circumstances in which the highest order of minds most frequently appear."

A very prolific source of evils to the offspring is found in early marrying. Females frequently enter the marital relation before the constitution is fully perfected in all its parts through the slow organizing processes of nature, which gives the organism health, strength, stamina, and longevity. Early child-bearing tends to hasten the constitution through the processes of maturation to a less perfect state of womanhood, in a period of life when the mother should yet be a girl; and she herself, being deficient in those essential qualities just enumerated, will not be able to transmit them to her offspring. Child-bearing and the rearing of children pertain to womanhood, and not to girlhood. As the age of maturity for women is twenty to twenty-five, there is a child-bearing period of twenty-five or thirty years. When a girl marries at the age of fifteen, she adds to this period ten years of the most important part of her existence. This time of life should be spent in active mental and physical exercise, that the organism may arrive at such a perfect state of development as will enable the female to endure the hardships and privations which attend the child-bearing woman. Youth is buoyant, full of hope, and lives in anticipation of great joy to be realized in the distant future. These stimulate the organism, and excite the formative processes which bring bodily health and knowledge—which make her an ornament in society; but these must, for the gratification of parent and lover, be supplanted by bodily infirmity and early decay, and the production of offspring with enfeebled constitutions.

PART II.

OF THE FŒTUS IN UTERO.

We are now to consider the fœtus in utero, the embryo of the infant, which is to be the object of the mother's love, of the father's affection, and of their common care. The intensity of this love is manifested in deep parental anxiety for the recovery of the sick babe; or in the grieved and broken hearts, when death, with his ruthless hands, takes it away.

Could the fœtus be the recipient of the same love and care, it would frequently be saved from many future evils. It is not, unfortunately, regarded as a thing of so much importance; but, that the mother may enjoy an evening's entertainment, a feast, a dance, or a fashionable dress, the fœtus must be subjected to influences which may affect it in the more advanced periods of its existence. And we know of no grounds of excuse, nor of aught in extenuation, of the criminality of the woman who wilfully subjects the being so carefully placed within her womb to agencies which are detrimental to its future happiness. In this enlightened age, ignorance is no excuse. The medical profession is ever ready to supply the requisite information, and has placed within the reach of all, such books as will afford valuable information, not only upon this, but other equally important points.

Parental love and affection are induced in a great degree by the dependence of the infant upon its parents for the supply of its necessities. This fact should direct more specific attention to the proper management of the mother through the term of pregnancy. During this time the fœtus is much more dependent. Its constitution is organizing. It is more susceptible to the effects of detrimental influences, which result in constitutional derangements. These facts make it imperative upon the mother to fully inform herself of the connection of the fœtus with her organism, and of the proper management of herself through the term of uterine gestation. This brings us to the consideration of the relation which exists between the mother and the *fœtus in utero*, and of the agencies which affect the latter through the organism of the mother.

For the better elucidation of the relation which exists between the mother and the fœtus, it is necessary to consider some of the laws of nutrition, and some of those which govern matter. There are many phenomena found in nature that are beyond the comprehension of man. We have in our gardens flowers in great variety, and vegetables of many kinds, growing from the same soil, and swayed by the same breezes; and we know not whence are the beauties of the rose, the savor of the berry, or the nourishing properties of the vegetable. But in the human structure there are tissues of a higher grade of organization, and of different kinds, as the brain, lung, muscle, bone, and nerve, which are germinated, developed, and maintained in a persistent, healthy state by the same circulating fluid—*the blood.* Not only the maintenance of a healthy state of the several tissues, but life itself depends upon the integrity of each of the constituents of the blood. It is then a matter of the highest importance for the blood to preserve its integrity, and to be ever ready to supply the several tissues with the *pabulum* appropriate to each. 'The importance of this condition of the blood to a persistent, healthy, state of the economy, is too great to be left to mere chance, and is, therefore, secured in those *self-formative* and self-sustaining powers which constitute it *the vital fluid.* Through this vitality, the blood is enabled to imbibe and to assimilate the material proper to its sustenance, and to eliminate all rejected matters through the emunctory functions of the several organs. This conservative power of the blood is sufficiently well established by physiological facts, and by results obtained from the administering of medicines. In addition to this, there are other facts which strongly support the doctrine of its conservative power; and these are, its ability to resist disease, and strong tendency to recover from a diseased to a normal state. Moreover, the blood makes forcible efforts to retain the peculiar type which characterizes families. In this we find the channel through which family traits and hereditary diseases, such as phthisis, cancer, and syphilis, pass through generations. So great, in fact, is the tendency of the blood to retain its type that, though these traits and diseases may meet with unfavorable circumstances for their development, and lie dormant through one or more generations, they finally reappear—constituting the phenomenon known in scientific language as *atavism*, and among stock-raisers as *breeding back.*

As we have already seen, the material condition of the germ depends upon the habitual state of the parents who supply its component parts. The material condition of matter is the state in which it naturally exists. But there are certain influences that can be brought to bear upon matter that will cause it to pass into other states, known as *dynamic conditions.* Thus, lead is, materially, a solid; whereas, in a melted state, it is, dynamically, a fluid body; and heat is the *dynamic force.* However often the lead may pass from one of these conditions to the other, there will be no change produced in either the metal or the heat. Such, however, is not the case with *organic* matter. When an egg is exposed to a high temperature, it will undergo such a change as will preclude the possibility of a return to its material, *original* condition. Therefore, every action belonging to living matter involves a change of structure, and this *change will increase with the growth of the body*, as an eschar produced upon the body of an infant will increase, *pari passu*, with the growth of its body. The blood, although a *fluid*, is susceptible to the effects of dynamic forces, which remain, as es chars, in the blood. Such is the explanation of the case of a man who, having a sixth finger on each hand, and a sixth toe on each foot, transmitted the deformities to a son, whose three sons, also, were characterized by the same deformities

We recognize our relation to surrounding objects by our senses; and, through these, impressions are made upon our organism, which vary greatly in character from each other—some being animating and wholesome; others displeasing, depressing, and even destructive to life itself. These impressions are received, and the effects are produced through the agency of the nervous system. Thus, grief and alarm have caused temporary derangements of the nervous system, and permanent lesions, such as issue in lunacy, idiocy, and death. In illustration of the effects of fear, Dr. Condie cites the case of a female child, who, having been repeatedly threatened by her parents with being given to a sweep to take away in his bag, on accidentally encountering a sweep who had entered the house in pursuit of his avocation, fell down immediately into a violent fit of convulsions, that terminated fatally in a few hours. Sir Astley Cooper refers to a case of a young girl who, for some offense, was put by a school mistress into a dark cellar. During the period of her incarceration, she was in a continued state of dreadful fright, and was returned to her parents in a similar but modified state. She passed a restless night, and in the morning was found to be laboring under fever. She constantly implored not to be put into the cellar. On the fourth day, Sir Astley Cooper saw the child, and, notwithstanding his efforts to relieve her, she was, three days afterwards, a corpse.* These are the effects of dynamic forces upon living matter; and it would be well, indeed, if these could be limited to the organism of the mother, and not involve the fœtus also.

The fœtus is enclosed in an organ richly endowed with nerves and blood-vessels, and obtains its nourishment directly from, and eliminates its effete matter through, the mother's blood. These facts make the fœtus, virtually, as much a part of her organization as her heart, lungs, or brain, and equally liable to the effects of dynamic forces to which

---

*For a history of these cases, see CONDIE on *Diseases of Children*.

the pregnant female is peculiarly liable. When we consider that the mother's organism has arrived at its fully-developed state, and power of resisting the effects of these forces, and contrast this state with the fœtus, we can understand the liability of the formative stage of the fœtus to affections, deformities, and to premature birth, as the results of dynamic force, though the mother herself may escape unharmed. This brings us to the consideration of the influences which affect the offspring through the organism of the mother, and they are the following:

A.—Alarm, dynamic force.

B.—Normal changes in the organism of the mother.

C.—Abnormal changes in the organism of the mother.

A.—There are various kinds of congenital deformities, and these consist of increased local vascularities, deposition of pigment and hair follicles, occasionally found upon the bodies of newly-born infants. These are supposed to be representations of an ax, a knife, a sword, an animal, or of some other object by which the mother had been frightened. Through a transient agitation, the implement or object had been physically photographed upon the body of the offspring. They are also supposed to represent different kinds of fruit, or other eatables, that the mother may have, through a morbid appetite, longed for. All this is contrary to physiological facts and correct observation, and is the popular, but erroneous, method of accounting for the so-called "mother's marks." The pregnant female is exposed to accidents occasioning great alarm, or to deep mental emotions, accompanied with great agitation of her nervous system, that will do as great violence to the fœtus, in the space of a few moments, as the slow process of enervation by disease in a long time. Should the fœtus survive the shock, it will suffer through life with some form of nervous derangement, and finally die with premature old age. These dynamic conditions are sometimes accompanied with local deformities. A very striking instance of this kind was told the author by an aged physician and friend, whose intelligence and purity of character place his statement far beyond question; and as it occurred in his father's family, there can be no mistake concerning the particulars. He says:

"A bee concealed in some honey my father was eating stung him on the tongue. This caused it to swell almost to suffocation. The unhappy circumstance took place, unfortunately, during the time my mother was pregnant with her second child. This child proved to be a sadly-afflicted son. His tongue was so much enlarged that he could not articulate a single word; nor could he control the saliva within his mouth, which caused a constant slabbering. He was mentally an imbecile, and died of premature old age at only *thirty years*. The immediate family, and both maternal and paternal ancestry were noted for their freedom from any hereditary tendencies whatever, and this is the only instance of the kind known to have occurred with any of their relatives. The mental affliction, the premature old age, and the deformity of the tongue, were, unquestionably, the results of the assigned cause."

The causes which bring like results to the fœtus are found not only in the home affairs of life, but under all circumstances which may surround the pregnant female. Hence, times of public danger afford illustrative casualties, of which the following is referred to by Dr. Combe, related by Baron Percy as having occurred after the siege of Landau, in 1793:

"In addition to a violent cannonading, which kept the women in a constant state of alarm, the arsenal blew up with a terrific explosion, which few could listen to with unshaken nerves. Out of ninety-two children born in the district within a few months afterwards, it is stated that sixteen died at the instant of birth; thirty-three languished for from eight to ten months after birth; eight became idiotic, and died before the age of five years, and two came into the world, with numerous fractures of the bones of the limbs, caused by the convulsive starts in the mother, excited by the cannonading and explosion."

Here, then, is a total of fifty-nine children out of ninety-two, or within a trifle of two out of every three, actually killed through the medium of the mother's alarm. It will be observed that, in every instance, the general system was affected, and there is no allusion to local manifestation, or such deformities as "*mother's marks;*" and this strictly accords with the physiological connection which exists between the mother and the fœtus. A correct understanding of this relation removes the grounds for attributing local deformities or "mother's marks" to the impressions of the instrument, or means by which the mother was frightened, or to any emotions of her mind or heart. This conclusion is further supported by the effects upon the human organization, of a constant state of apprehension of evil. This retards the progress of nutrition and development, and is supposed to cause a total arrest of these functions, and induce gangrene and death. A case of this kind is related by M. Ridard:*

"A man, thirty years of age, was affected with stone in the bladder, and saw a patient die by his side after being operated up for the same complaint. His imagination became excited, his thoughts being constantly fixed upon the operation which he himself expected to undergo, and upon the probable death that would follow; and the result was, that without any operation at all, he died at the end of a month, affected with gangrene of both penis and scrotum."

Dr. Carpenter says:

"Hence, also, it is that the morbid feelings of the hypochondriac, who is constantly directing his attention to his own fancied ailments,

* CARPENTER's *Principles of Physiology.*

tend to induce real disorders in the action of the organs which are supposed to be affected."

In the same category, too, may be placed those instances (to which any value may be attached) wherein a strong and persistent impression upon the mind of the mother, has appeared to produce a corresponding effect upon the development of the *fœtus in utero*. In this case, the effect (if admitted to be really exerted) must be produced upon the maternal *blood*, and transmitted through it to the fœtus, since there is no nervous communication between the parent and the offspring.

B.—As we advance from infancy to old age, the organism passes through successive changes induced by development, education, and experience in the affairs of life; thus,

> "The tear down childhood's cheek that flows,
> Is like the dew-drop on the rose;
> When next the summer breeze comes by,
> And waves the bush, the flower is dry."

> "Youth is ever apt to judge in haste,
> And lose the medium in the wild extreme."

> "These are the effects of doting age,
> Vain doubts, and idle cares, and over-caution."

The character of these changes is determined, in a great measure, by the influences which are brought to bear upon the individual, and in a manner that, "If a reflective, aged man, were to find at the bottom of an old trunk, where it had lain forgotten fifty years, a record, which he had written of himself when he was young, simply and vividly describing his whole heart and pursuits, and reciting *verbatim* many passages of the language which he sincerely uttered, would he not read it with as much wonder as if it had come to him from the dead? He would surely half lose the sense of his identity under the impression of this dissimilarity. It would appear as if it must be the tale of the juvenile days of some ancestor, with whom he had no connection but that of name. He would feel that the young man thus introduced to him was separated by so wide a distance of character as to render all congenial association or connection impossible. At every sentence he would be tempted to repeat: 'Foolish youth, I have no sympathy with your feelings; I can hold no converse with your understanding!' Thus, you see, that in the course of a long life a man may experience several moral individualities different from each other; that, if you could find a real individual that would fulfil the characteristics of these stages in their several developments down to the last, and then bring them all together into one society, as the representatives of the successive stages of one man, they would feel themselves a most heterogeneous party, would oppose and probably despise one another, and soon after separate, not caring ever to meet again. If the dissimilarity in mind were as great as in person, there would in both respects be a most striking contrast between the youth of seventeen and the sage of seventy. The one of these contrasts, an old, man might contemplate, if he had a true portrait for which he had sat in the bloom of his life, and should hold it before a mirror in which he beholds his present countenance; and the other he would powerfully feel, if he had such a genuine and detailed memoir as I have supposed." If it were possible for the circumstances of home, and of public affairs, and the state of science under which a child might be born, to continue uninterruptedly through life; his organism would pass through less and fewer changes than under the ever-changing affairs of human existence. Therefore, the greater the vicissitudes of a given family, the greater will be the difference in those children born at the extreme periods of the parents' life. These differences may be regarded as the expression of the several changes through which the parents may have passed. If the truth of this is admitted, it becomes a matter of the highest importance to pay due regard to the character of the influences which are brought to bear upon ourselves—and especially those to which our children are subjected.

C.—The abnormal conditions of the system are caused by disease, the loss of near relatives, adverse circumstances, or a constant state of expectation of evil. These abnormities become more manifest in pregnancy, because the vital organs are more active in the performance of their functions, and the maternal instinct is being strongly developed. The sensitive* state of the mother is, at this crisis, peculiarly intensified. To illustrate, we will suppose a young and healthy woman marries at the usual time of life, and, in due time, becomes a mother. The child proves all that the fond parents desire, and its system shows no indications of organic derangement whatever. After this first delivery, the mother's health begins to decline. The *second* child is born. It is puny, and continues in a delicate state through youth; and in manhood is stunted in body and cramped in intellect. The *third* is as well developed as the *first;* but in after life is afflicted with some form of nervous derangement.

---

*This increased sensitiveness of the female is sometimes taken advantage of in the maltreatment of the pregnant female for the gratification of a malicious spirit.

The *fourth* survives the periods of early life, but suffers from indigestion, and is a prey to nervous excitement. The fifth is still-born. After this, the mother's health being in an improved condition, she gives birth to the *sixth* child, which suffers with convulsive disorders in childhood, and in after life possesses a nervous excitability of temperament, which no regimen can palliate or remove. Finally, under a recovered state of health, she bears children that are of the type of the first born. Such conditions of the mother during the child-bearing period determine the destinies of her offspring. The prime cause of the normal and abnormal conditions of the members of the same family may be traced to like conditions of the mother's organism previous to, and during the time of, her different pregnancies.

From the foregoing, and from what is known upon this subject, we may conclude, *first*, that the habitual psychical and physical state of both parents prior to, and at the time of conception, exercise a marked influence upon the general system of the offspring; *second*, that during the entire term of gestation, the fœtus receives the material for its formative processes directly from the blood of the mother, and the integrity of this fluid depends on the state of her own assimilative processes, digestion, secretion, and excretion, and that these are influenced by her own mental state. Hence, those slowly-enervating influences arising either from physical derangement, or from unhappy conditions of life that disturb the mental state of the mother, also materially affect the general system of the offspring; *third*, that an immediate and violent shock to the mental and nervous system of the mother will so affect her blood as to retard or pervert the developing processes of the fœtus; and when this occurs in the early months of pregnancy, there may be a malformation effected in addition to the retarded development and nervous disorder, as was the case with the child in the instance of the bee-sting.

From the foregoing, we discover the maternal influence upon the fœtus to be constitutional in its effects, rather than productive of local deformities, called "*mother's marks.*" Therefore, keeping this in view, we perceive the great importance to the female of a healthy state of body and mind at the time of conception and during the term of uterine gestation. This requires a proper observance of all the conditions upon which the preservation of this state depends. Among these may be mentioned *associations*, mental and physical exercise, food, and dress.

OF ASSOCIATIONS.

The necessity of the mother's amicable relation to her associates, especially to those of her household, has already been referred to in this part. In addition to this, I remark that her companions should be such as will help her to diminish any deficiences which mar her happiness, and divert her attention from anything which would be detrimental to an even, healthy state of her mind and body. The mother herself should guard against those ill-tempered feelings and emotions which are sometimes excited by the pregnant state, and also remember the great difference between the placid and amiable disposition of the agreeable housewife, and the turbulent spirit of the house-brawler, who is the cause of much unhappiness. The statesman may also ask, with great propriety—Is she not also the remote cause of much national discontent and disorder? To the former class of mothers we are to look for domestic happiness and national content.

OF MENTAL AND PHYSICAL EXERCISE.

There are few persons who are not competent to devise a plan, or to execute one which is already devised; but to be able to devise, and then to execute, requires a combination of faculties which few persons possess by nature, or have acquired by persevering industry. These faculties are named, respectively, the inventive and the constructive. In the combination of them resides the highest degree of *mental* and *physical development*, and the loftiest grade of usefulness. The coöperation of the two faculties is more than useful, inasmuch as it animates the mind and stimulates the bodily functions. Thus the individual receives a life-renewing impulse. The spirits are saved from sadness and gloom, and the system can more effectually resist the encroachments of disease. The joint exercise of the faculties of invention and construction lead to the cultivation of many pursuits of pleasure and of profit, such as the rearing of flowers, the domestication of animals, the cutting and making of dresses, and last, *not least*, the ART and *practice* of *cookery*—a thorough knowledge of which constitutes the *highest* and *most useful accomplishment* a woman can attain. The woman who occupies her time in this way, combined with a modicum of religious and secular reading, is contented and happy, beautiful and useful in her home, however humble it may be; and her children will be *born* in those "*circumstances*" most favorable to the production of healthy constitutions, amiable dispositions, and the highest order of intellectual endowments.

OF THE FOOD.

There is nothing of greater importance in conducting the female through the term of pregnancy than the due nourishment of her physical economy. This is of prime importance, not only to the mother's health, to her safe delivery and good getting up, but also to the proper development of the fœtus and its continued well-being in after life. So much depends upon the proper nourishment of the female through the term of pregnancy that she should, to some extent, be informed of the physiology of digestion, absorption and assimilation. These can not be fully treated of here; but there are some particulars which can not be passed over, in justice to the aim of our work, and they are these:

1st. The elaboration of matter for the remarkable increase in size of the uterus, which takes place *pari passu* with the development of the fœtus, and for the growth of the latter.

2d. The elimination of the carbonaceous matter of the fœtus through the mother's physical economy.

3d. The imparting to the mother's blood of excrementitious matter other than the carbon.

1st. When an organ ceases its secretive function, the remaining healthy organ will supply the deficiency to the economy by taking upon itself an increased activity in the performance of its function. This same law operates in the digestive organs when additional material is demanded for the construction of the new being. This gives rise to an increased appetite and a demand for a more liberal diet. Such is the case with the healthy female who maintains the demand, by a continuance of her daily physical exertions, for the accustomed amount of food to supply the waste of her own body, and whose organs continue in the daily performance of their functions. When a due relation between the appetite and the powers of digestion is maintained, through the term of pregnancy, there is a healthy state, but when, from any cause whatever, the healthy state of this relation is disturbed, evil results must ensue. One of these causes is found in the encumbered state of the mother, in the latter months of pregnancy, from the enlargement of the uterus and the heaviness of its contents. This prevents her from taking the accustomed exercise; consequently the demand for nourishment to supply the waste of her own economy is greatly diminished, and, if the appetite continues unabated, its indulgence will result in derangement of the digestive organs, accompanied with heart-burn, nausea, flatulence, constipation and a sense of general fullness. The *ingesta* is now imperfectly elaborated and the organism insufficiently nourished. From this state of the system arises a constant craving for food and confectionaries, and the indulgence of the female in these excesses will increase the fullness to oppression, and if this is not relieved by art, nature will endeavor to do so by bleeding from one of the mucous membranes. This hemorrhage sometimes takes place from the uterus. In this event the life of the fœtus is endangered by a premature birth, and the mother is subjected to serious risk from flooding. It is true that the suppression of the menses contributes to the growth of the fœtus, but the amount is small, not more than one pound of organized matter, while the fœtus and the growth of the womb, and the formation of the placenta, will amount to fourteen pounds. Hence there will remain thirteen pounds of new growth to be provided for by the digestive organs of the mother in the short space of nine months.

2d. The elimination of carbonaceous matter, *after birth*, takes place through the lungs, and is brought thither by the blood from every part of the body. It is different, however, with the *fœtus*. Its lungs do not, as yet, perform their physiological functions. Its blood is diverted from them by arrangement, to the placenta, which may be called the *fœtal lung*, as it performs a similar function. This organ is attached to the uterus by tufts, which permit the placental veins to bathe freely in the blood of the mother, as do the gills of fish in surrounding water. And according to the same law the excrementitious matter of fœtal blood is imparted to the purer blood of the mother, and receives oxygen in return. The fœtal stomach, like its lungs, does not, as yet, perform its function; hence the placenta is a substitute also for the alimentary canal as a means of supplying to the blood, nourishment for the fœtus. The blood thus purified and laden with fresh stores returns to the fœtus, circulates through its capillary system, deposits the necessary material for its growth, takes up the waste matter, and returns to the placenta with impurities to be again imparted to the blood of the mother. The carbon being the most important of these impurities, we particularly allude to it at present. The increased carbon in the blood renders the blood thick,*

---

*The author was, upon one occasion, called to relieve the sufferings of a lady in the seventh month of her pregnancy. who was suffering with a derangement of the digestive organs, accompanied with a sense of fullness, as above described. There was a general pallor, attended with a sense of suffocation. It was apprehended that the blood was too thick to circulate freely through the capillary system. As a means of relief a small quantity, *a gill*, of thick, tarry blood was drawn from the arm, which, notwithstanding the smallness of the quantity, caused her to faint. A few days' abstinence from food, with opening medicines, the blood recovered its natural fluid form, and the patient recovered to as comfortable a condition as could be expected for one in her condition, and after her confinement presented her husband with twins—*two unusually large boys.*

and gives it a tarry appearance. This increased consistency retards circulation through the capillaries and prevents, in part, those metamorphic changes from taking place which are needful to the due nourishment of the economy. And finally, these result in derangement and disease which require medical treatment. The derangements thus produced are mainly those of the nervous system and of the digestive organs. The former, is in consequence of the nerve centers not receiving the necessary stimulus from the sluggish flow of the blood, and the latter, results from the deteriorated quality of the gastric, pancreatic, and biliary secretions, by which the digestive processes are more imperfectly performed. These conditions still further deteriorate the blood, and the economy is more inefficiently nourished. Under these circumstances, the free indulgence of a morbid appetite is like adding fuel to flame.

But when the economy is invaded by a disturbing cause, we must not be unmindful of the fact that nature is ever upon the watch, ready to assert the supremacy of her laws; hence, she imposes upon the lungs an increased action in the performance of their function—as when one lung, or one kidney, compensates for the impaired utility of its fellow. It occasionally happens, however, that she is not adequate to the emergencies of the case, and assistance must then be supplied by due attention to the diet, to the manner of dress, and by the institution of such medical treatment as the nature of the case may demand.

3d. The presence of waste matters in the system is highly prejudicial to good health, and for this reason there is ample provision made for their elimination. The bowels, kidneys, lungs, and skin, discharge their respective secretions. By the obstruction of any of these organs, the secretion accumulates within the system, unless thrown off by some other organ. The skin and mucous membrane sometimes perform this adventitious function. There are agencies which excite an increased action of these membranes and cause them to eliminate an increased amount of animal matter. Of these agencies a heated and confined atmosphere is among the most efficient. Many persons have experienced the ill effects of inhaling the breath and effluvia from the bodies of others. These effects are not only due to the carbonic acid gas, but also to animal matter of which the effluvium is partly composed. The inhalation of carbonic acid gas produces a sense of suffocation; whereas, the animal matter causes nausea and vomiting. The sickening odor arising from freshly-drawn blood is due to the animal matter. This fluid is used in sugar refineries for clarifying sugar; and when a fresh quantity is introduced into hot syrup, the animal effluvia is so offensive that the rooms are almost uninhabitable for several hours afterward. The exhalation from the human body is necessarily contaminated with animal matter; and that from each individual seems to possess properties peculiar to itself. This enables the dog to trace his master among the footsteps of many persons. The occurrence of scarlatina, measles, etc., among school-children and students at college, is due to the intermingling of these different matters, like salts of different metals, which, when their solutions are mixed, form precipitates of new compounds, differing in their physical and chemical properties from the original salts.

The facts just cited respecting the effluvia from the adult organism equally apply to the fœtus. All its glandular systems are actively producing their secretions. This is evidenced by the existence of bile and mucus in the bowels, urine in the bladder, and the sebaceous matter—*vernix caseosa*—which covers the body of the newly-born. The peculiar situation of the fœtus renders it impossible for these secretions to be removed directly from the body of the fœtus in like manner as after its birth; hence there must be some other provision made for their removal, else fœtal existence would be of short duration, if it could exist at all. This provision is found, *first*, in the chemical composition of the fœtal effete matters, as differing from those of the adult; *secondly*, in their being in part taken up by the blood of the mother and eliminated through the emunctories of her economy. These we will consider as:

(*a.*) *The alvine dejections.* There is a marked difference in the physical and chemical constituents of the fæces of the fœtus and that of the delivered body. The former is a blackish green, viscid, inodorous matter, composed of mucus secreted by the intestinal mucus membrane, mingled with bile, and is called meconium. It neither contains the animal matter excretions, nor does it possess other important characteristics which are peculiar to the latter. These the fœtus imparts to the blood of the mother, and, when retained in her system, she is a fit subject for the reception of disease.

(*b.*) In consequence of the little practical importance of a knowledge of the physiological and pathological conditions of the urine of the fœtus, it has not received the same attention from physiologists and chemists as that of the child or man. But it is shown that the constituents of the one are very different from those of the other. Urea, the nitrogenized compound which characterizes the urine of the delivered, does not exist in that of the fœtus; but, instead of it, there are two nitrogenized compounds, *allantoin* and *albumen*, which do not belong to the healthy urine of the former.

I cannot speak positively as to the character of the former of these substances, but regard it as strongly resembling the latter. It does not readily decompose, nor is it inimical to life, as is urea. Were it not for this provision against the formation of urea, fœtal existence would be of short duration; its death would ensue from *uraemic* poisoning.

(*c.*) The skin of the fœtus also performs its function quite actively. This is evidenced by the quantity of sebaceous matter usually found upon the cutaneous surface of the newly-born infants. This is an oleaginous substance and is designed to lubricate the skin. The accumulation and retention of this lubricate are not inimical to the health of the fœtus, hence its removal is not provided for, and there is time enough after birth, as a matter of cleanliness. In these provisions for the preservation of the fœtus we discover marked indications of the conservatism of natural law and the workings of an omniscient Creator. It occasionally occurs in the latter months of pregnancy that the organs of the mother do not perform their eliminative functions sufficiently active when the effete matters of her own system, as well as those of the fœtus, are permitted to accumulate in her blood. This accumulation will give rise to much inconvenience, which will demand prompt relief, as in the case already cited.

OF DRESS.

Of the conditions and necessities of the female which are essential to the well-being of the offspring there are none more important and more under the control of her own will than the manner in which she should wear her clothes. An *improper manner of dressing is one of those things which has contributed largely to the perils of child-bearing*, and has induced some authors to believe and teach that pregnancy and childbirth are pathological or diseased conditions of the female, and not physiological or healthy processes. This, however, is a mistake. Pregnancy and child-bearing are not diseases, nor do they partake of the nature of them. They are the means by which the race is propagated, and, consequently, must be governed by natural and conservative laws which have regard to both mother and offspring. Were these conditions of the female pathological in character it would be a perversion of natural and conservative laws, whereby the end in view would be defeated, the world could never have been peopled; but, as it is, child-bearing is conducive to female longevity, and the world is peopled. Hence we may conclude that conception, pregnancy and child-bearing are the results of the generative organs *when in the active performance of their physiological functions*.

If the pregnant female could ouly appreciate the reality of these facts, she would be relieved of those grave and unfounded apprehensions, which induce her to regard the issue of her anticipated confinement as more than doubtful. This appreciation would not only dispel her fears and anxieties, but also cause her to take a more rational view of her situation. It would make her happy and cheerful. She would endeavor to inform herself of the nature of those laws of child-bearing, that the manner of her living may be more in compliance with their demands.

Although science and common sense have done much

in reforming the manner of female dress, yet the natural laws of health are frequently violated by the vain endeavor to improve the forms which nature beautifies without any such assistance. The modern manner of dressing was not the means by which the ancient Greeks and Romans acquired their classic forms. It was by means which permitted free and easy movements of the joints and muscles. The axis of the spine was erect, with its natural and graceful curves; the shoulders were square, and the breast arched with a perfect symmetry. They permitted their muscles to develop. This gave them ease and grace of movement, as well as speedy action. It also gave them that rotundity of contour which is so beautiful to the eye.

The contrasting of two drawings—one representing a well-formed female, with the various organs in their natural position, and the other representing one who has become deformed, and the organs displaced by tight lacing, steel stays, and walking the Grecian-bend—would demonstrate so great a variety of evils, that a special chapter would be required for their elucidation. We will not, however, give the subject so much space, but will mention a few of the most important evils from this cause: *First*, undue pressure of the body is a prolific cause of determination of blood to the brain, and may be the exciting cause of disease of this organ; *second*, the action of the heart and blood-vessels is not so free and easy; *third*, the blood cannot flow sufficiently free through the capillaries, thereby preventing the nourishment and development of the parts; *fourth*, the respiratory organs are so compressed as to interfere with the breathing process—for this cause the female cannot take that degree of exercise which is essential to health; *fifth*, pressure upon the mammary glands will either cause absorption or disease of the organs; *sixth*, pressure over the stomach and bowels will arrest the peristaltic movements, thereby causing imperfect digestion and constipation of the bowels; *seventh*, the uterus will be forced down, making a case of prolapsus uteri. Walking the Grecian-bend greatly promotes this displacement by lessening the lumbar curve of the spine, which brings the pelvic plane more horizontal by taking away the support which the organ receives from the pelvic arch and abdominal walls.

From a consideration of the foregoing evils, which result from an improper mode of dressing, it would seem to be the dictates of true philosophy to avoid them, and act in strict compliance with the demands of the human body. There should not be those infringements upon the organism, which not only impair the health, but are also the remote cause of tardy and difficult labor. But philosophy, reason, common sense, good health, and the welfare of the offspring, are all sacrificed to the modern usages imposed upon the female. She cannot, unaided, stem the tide of fanaticism which deluges the fashionable world. She must be supported by father and brother, husband and son; and, by not discharging this duty, they become likewise responsible for the evils incurred.

Except in instances involving right and wrong, decencies and indecencies, our ideas of elegance of dress and of beauty are matters of taste and of education. The Jew, the Greek and the Roman each had his ideas of elegance, and regarded his own style of dress and of female beauty as superior to any other. In order to produce a successful revolution in any one of the usages of society, public opinion must be in its favor, and, as the mode of dressing is conventional, let that opinion approve of the manner of the ancients, who wore their garments by straps passing over the shoulders, and not with a cincture around the waist, which, with the weight of the garments suspended, compress the abdominal, the spinal and the thoracic muscles. The effect of this continued pressure is the attenuation of these muscles, which deprives the female, to some extent, of their assistance in the expulsive effort of child-birth. The want of this assistance is often the cause of much inconvenience and suffering.

Could a woman only know how absolutely ridiculous she appeared while making strenuous, and frequently *painful*, efforts in the preparation of her dressing, and in distorting her body to some fashionable method of walking—as *the Grecian-bend*—to bring about the evils we have just enumerated, she would not be long in loosening her stays, and in assuming the erect posture, *as designed by nature*. The following case of death from tight-lacing, with post mortem results, as reported in the *London Lancet*, will farther illustrate the evils which result from this pernicious practice, and also show that the foregoing is not a fancy sketch, but sad reality:

"Jemima H——, aged twenty (appeared to me to be twenty-four), servant, complained, on returning from an errand, of some headache and intense feeling of cold, about 2 P. M., on December 21st last. Her mistress desired her to lie down for the remaining part of the afternoon, but the headache still persisted, and she was permitted to retire to bed for the night. As she did not "put in an appearance" at her usual hour the following morning, the mistress went to her room for the purpose of inquiring the cause, when she found the patient still dressed, as on the previous evening, lying on the bed, and quite incapable of being aroused. I was sent for at 7:30

A. M., and found her insensible on the bed, with all her clothes on, dressed, her face pale, pupils widely dilated, breathing stertorous, and on trying to remove her clothing, the task proved to be so difficult a one that I was obliged to cut it off. I then considered the symptoms (from the meagre and faulty history) due to congestion of the brain membranes, arising, probably, from the intense cold of the night, acting on a weak heart. Some diffusible stimulant was ordered, if it could be taken, and fly-blisters to the nape of the neck and extremities. I then left. At 10 A. M., the hour of my second visit, the patient was wildly delirious, unrestrainable, and powerfully convulsed (clonic). At 2 P. M. I was informed, on again visiting her, she had died a short time previous, after a violent convulsive seizure, apparently exhausted. She was removed that night to the public mortuary, to await a coroner's order for post mortem examination. There was no history to the case, save the evidence of the mistress, given at the inquest, which went to prove that she had frequently, but unavailingly, remonstrated with the girl for her persistent folly in lacing so tightly.

"*Autopsy* (forty-two hours after death): Weather intensely cold; air crispy, dry; sky clear; recent snow-fall. *Rigor mortis* complete; no marks of violence; body indifferently nourished. I was at once struck with the nude configuration of the body, which was peculiar from the extraordinary amount of constriction at the loins, and the "squareness" of the shoulders, which were remarkably high for a delicately-formed female, the clavicles being horizontal, straight, transversely, the form of the upper part of the body being flat and triangular, the base being formed by the square shoulders, the apex resting on the pelvis, which projected considerably, and the sides perfectly free from contour, and sharply defined. There was little pectoral or mammal development; the lower extremities were œdematous, and the whole appearance gave me the unpleasant impression of being pinched. On opening the chest, the lungs were found to fill the cavity completely; the right lung was adherent throughout to the chest walls, and congested; the left lung also congested. Pleural cavity contained some fluid, but there were no adhesions. The position of the diaphram corresponded to that of extreme expiration.

Heart very small; did not weigh more than four ounces, and flabby; structure pale and weak; right ventricle distended with black fluid blood; left valves healthy; pericardium contained about three-quarters of an ounce of fluid. Abdomen contained over a pint of serum in peritoneal cavity. Liver enormously enlarged, congested and friable, the capsule readily tearing off; it extended completely across the abdomen, overlapping the left margin of the spleen, to which it was firmly adherent, compressing the stomach, duodenum, transverse colon, and small intestines. I should think it did not weigh less than between sixty and sixty-five ounces; gall bladder, distended with bile, descending an inch below superior margin of liver. Stomach very small, not larger than an infant's; walls hypertrophied; rugæ considerably enlarged, and contained some dark fluid, apparently coffee. Duodenum much thickened; contained some bile and digested food, as did small intestines. Spleen and kidneys intensely congested and enlarged. Brain membranes intensely congested. I do not think I have ever seen them more so. The whole surface presented the appearance of a blackened mass, almost unrecognizable. There was an apoplectic spot on the surface of the right hemisphere posteriorly, with some effusions of lymph. The brain substance was considerably softer than in health, and presented a "mottled" appearance on being cut into. No fluid in ventricles. Dark-colored fluid at base of brain. Sinuses engorged, as also *vena galeni.**

It is true this is an extreme case, and no argument is needed to show that the death, the displacement of the several organs and their diseased conditions, as demonstrated by the post mortem examination, were the effects of the assigned cause; hence no comments are needed but to meet the anticipated response, "Oh! I do not lace so tight as that," forgetting that injury is done in proportion to the tightness of the lacing. For a perfectly healthy state of the organs *they must not be compressed at all.*

---

*See July number of the *London Lancet*, 1871. The case is reported by W. H. Sheehy, L. R. C. P. Ed., etc.

Keeping in view the dependence of the fœtus upon the continued good health of the mother for its growth and development of a vigorous constitution, and that the processes of child-bearing are normal, and not abnormal, we now remark that it involves an increased activity, not only of the generative organs, but also of the *vital* organs of the mother's economy. *This increased activity implies an increased draft upon the capacity of these organs, and this increased draft implies an increased demand upon the vital forces, and this increased demand implies an increased necessity for observing all the conditions and obeying all the laws essential to the maintenance of health.*

As the *vital forces* derive their stimulus from wholesome food, pure air, and exercise, the pregnant female must not, to the exclusion of these, be considered an invalid—to eat dainties, to lie supinely, and to breathe impure air, but let the usual course of life be continued without any sudden or radical change in her customs and habits. When any article of diet is found to produce unpleasant results let it be removed from the diet list.

The mother may not only exercise herself within doors, but also in the open air, either by walking or riding in a carriage, avoiding jolting and jarring. The continuance of a walk, a ride, or of any other kind of exercise, so far as to produce fatigue, is frequently followed by serious consequences; therefore, she should not be subjected to fatiguing or exhausting efforts of either body or mind. The hour for exercising in the open air is to be determined by the climate, the location and the general health of the mother. As these are so varied, it is impossible to indicate one which would be alike appropriate in every instance; but the following will, to some extent, indicate the proper time for her walks and rides. Our space will not admit of a full history of the effects of cold upon the human economy; but suffice to say that, when the mother is enjoying good health, exercise in a cold atmosphere for a short time will produce a temporary depression, followed by a healthy reaction and beneficial results; whereas a prolonged exposure will produce a continued depression, followed by an unhealthy reaction and grave results. Therefore she should not, during the cold seasons, exercise too freely in the open air, and not then in the mornings and in the evenings, but with proper wrappings and overshoes, let mid-day supply the desired hour.

One of the most hurtful influences is *miasm*. This gaseous poison is generated from decomposing vegetable matter exposed to moisture and a due amount of solar heat. It is produced in such quantities in some localities as to entitle them to the appellation of *miasmatic districts*, from whence it is diffused through the air, and when it is inhaled into the lungs and absorbed by the skin, it causes miasmatic diseases, which are of the intermittent and congestive forms. As Spring is its favored season, and is accompanied by a damp atmosphere, the female should avoid the morning fogs and evening dews of the Spring months.

Under ordinary circumstances the observance of all the conditions and laws upon which health depends is essential to its maintenance. But the increased activity of the various organs consequent upon the pregnant state necessitates, as we have already seen, an increased vigilance in the observance of these conditions and laws. Habits of cleanliness, not only of the body and clothing, but also of the bed and of the apartments, should be strictly observed. By due attention to these, with well-ventilated rooms, the animal effluvia arising from the body and from the lungs are more readily dissipated, the body is invigorated, the mind is made cheerful and the spirits happy. In conclusion, we may observe that the ills of child-bed are not by any means necessary attendants. They are often the results of the mismanagement of the female, either during the term of pregnancy, in her delivery, or during the lying-in month.

PART III.

MANAGEMENT OF THE NEWLY-BORN.

The changes which the constitution undergoes in its transit through the periods of life, demand corresponding observances for the maintenance of health. It is, therefore, necessary to study the laws of health in relation to each of the periods of human existence. We have treated of the means by which an infant may be born with an organization capable of being developed into a healthy and vigorous constitution. The next topic is infantile existence.

The treatment which the offspring meets with upon entering the world, depends upon the degree of intelligence and moral worth of the parents. With the unchristianized, it is the victim of the most revolting practices. The cannibal will sacrifice his babe to his appetite. The inhabitants of India will sacrifice their babes to appease their gods. It was a practice among the Romans to leave it to the arbitrary will of the father, whether his newly-born should survive, or be left in the street to perish. The aim of the Spartans was to train it to be a soldier, and to this end they endeavored to make it capable of great endurance of heat, of cold, and of bodily affliction. Among their laws was one requiring parents to bring their babes to a place called *Lesche*, to be examined by the heads of the clans, or the most ancient men of the tribe, who, upon finding them of a feeble organization, or deformed, gave directions for their destruction by throwing them into a cavern called *Apothetæ*. If the infant was possessed of a good organization, and not deformed, it was returned to the parents, and orders issued for its education and for its reception of one of the nine thousand shares of land. THE CHRISTIAN IS THE HIGHEST ORDER OF NATION—THE CHRISTIAN IS THE HIGHEST ORDER OF MAN. *We therefore rear and educate our children to the* HIGHEST PURPOSE OF MAN, *and this requires thorough physical, mental, and moral training.*

Birth is that act which terminates the intra-uterine life of the infant, and ushers it into an extra-uterine existence. This event places the infant in contact with very different surroundings. From within its closed matrix, from its immersion in water, from a higher and an even temperature, from a dormant state of the five senses, from inaction of several of the organs in the performance of their functions, a being is at once ushered into a dry atmosphere, to a lower and an uneven temperature, to an excited state of the five senses, and to action of several of the organs in the performance of their functions. Thus, its entrance into the world is marked with an organization which will enable it to maintain an independent existence. The various faculties are now to be exercised. The first impression of sound is to be made upon the ear, of light upon the eye, of touch upon the skin, of heat and of cold upon the cutaneous nerves, of food upon the palate, and of odors upon the olfactory nerves. Were it possible for an adult to undergo so sudden and so great a transition as this, it is possible that the shock would prove fatal to his life. If the fœtal brain were sufficiently developed to be conscious of the transition, the same result might be anticipated. But this was foreseen by the Creator, and hence the brain is only developed enough to be able to preside over the feeble fœtal organization.

It is not so far developed in its newly-born state as to enable it to be conscious of its necessities. Instinctive desires, and reflex action of the nervous system, are the agencies by which its feeble vitality is manifested. They are also the agencies by which the organic functions are excited to action. In addition to the feebleness of the brain, the nerve textures and the muscular and membraneous tissues are extremely delicate, and the bones are soft and flexible. The infant, then, is not only unconscious of its necessities, but is physically incapable of supplying the least of its wants. It comes into the world as an object of our care. We are not only to supply the necessities of life, but we are to secure to it, at the time of its birth, those circumstances which are most compatible with its organization. The "*little stranger*" should, therefore, meet with those conditions that are as similar as possible to those of its former state of existence. The senses must not be subjected to marked impressions, but gradually become inured to the performance of their functions. The sense of touch is the first to be exercised. Although the *vernix caseosa* is some protection to the cutaneous nerves, yet the most delicate of textures with which it is possible for the infant to come in contact, is rough and harsh in comparison with its former smooth and watery place of abode

When the infant is handed to the nurse, it is usually received upon a shawl or blanket, regardless of the coarseness of texture, or of the smoothness of the surface—as though anything would do to wrap the baby in. But instead of such rough textures, there should be provided a piece of new canton flannel, of sufficient size to envelop the babe. Even this is not sufficient to protect it from cold, and to keep it at an even temperature. The necessary additional wrappings will be determined by the season of the year and the temperature of the room.

The mechanical impressions made upon the cutaneous nerves are of less importance, however, than those made by the coldness of an atmosphere of sixty or seventy degrees, compared with the higher and more even temperature of the womb. The atmosphere coming in contact with the body, and in close proximity to the blood by inhalation, along with the evaporation from the body, rapidly reduces the temperature and depresses the vital forces. These degrees of temperature are higher than are usually met with by the newly-born; hence it is that there are more infants still-born in the colder than in the warmer seasons of the year. The feeble organization of the newly-born is incapable of maintaining the higher degrees of heat imparted by the mother's economy, and its capacity is lessened by the fatigue of the labor, and the pressure to which the brain was subjected during the act of birth. Under these depressing influences, the infant cannot long survive its struggles for existence. The lower animals instinctively act upon these facts; and it is well to remark the wonderful care they exercise in protecting their young—not only from extreme cold, but from chilling influences. When young birds are removed from their nests, their temperature rapidly declines; and when the young of carnivorous animals are kept with the mother, they lose only about three degrees of heat; whereas, when they are removed from the parent, their temperature will fall several degrees lower. It is the result of daily observation, that heat and its maintenance at an even temperature is not only essential to germination and reproduction in both the vegetable and animal kingdoms, but also to health development, and the prolonging of life. Notice the florist in his greenhouse—the *care* with which he *nurses* the *tender plants*. He has constant regard to the temperature of the nourishing air and water. Hence the thermometer and the fire when chilling winter, with his icy hand, brings the hoary frost. Then turn to the newly-born and helpless infants entwining themselves around the parental heart, and observe—in consequence of their delicate organization—the easy susceptibility to the effects of cold. We should then observe, with greater care, the temperature of our offspring, their surrounding atmosphere, their food, and their drink.

From the inception of the prolific germ of the fœtus until its maturity at birth, it is kept at 100 degrees temperature (Fahr). A variation of a few degrees below this point would retard its development, or blast its existence. Then, taking nature as our guide, and knowing the normal temperature of our body to be ninety-eight degrees, let this temperature be maintained from the cradle to the grave. And as the debilitating influences of early life and of old age are inimical to the maintenance of the normal temperature, these must be compensated by additional clothing, and avoiding exposure to cold. With barbarous cruelty, some parents try to "*harden*" their infants and children to the endurance of cold—a cruel idea that hardens many children into the grave, or sows in them the seed of disease and early decay.

When the vital forces are actively exercising themselves in a healthy and vigorously-constituted individual, during the middle periods of life, the power of resisting the consequences of exposure to cold is at its acme. From these periods, it *shades* off to the *extremes* of life—infancy and old age. It is not exposure to cold, nor the power of resisting the consequences of such exposure, that makes a healthy and vigorous constitution; but it is the accumulated effects of successive exposures that enervate and ruin such a constitution. In proof of this, it is a well-known fact that, during the late war, those men whose avocations were sedentary and in-doors, as clerks and students, after becoming somewhat inured to the hardships of the soldiers' life, made more efficient and enduring soldiers than those taken from such pursuits as exposed them to the inclemency of the weather—farmers, for instance.

With infants and children, constitutions are not made, but *are to be formed*. If exposures are enervating and ruinous to constitutions already formed, how much more so are they to those that are in process of formation? In the young, they not only bring about the immediate and remote consequences that the adult incurs, but the constitutions in their formative processes are stunted; and those children, at maturity, *will be mentally and physically dwarfed*. Heat and its maintenance at a uniform temperature, are so essential to the development, growth, and preservation of health in the fœtus, the infant, and the adult, that nature provides means for its evolution, and carefully regards the uniformity of its temperature. But the "*all-wise*" MAN, in his self-sufficiency, says to her, *This is, and this is not.* Hence, the exposures and variations from the degree of heat that nature, in her most emphatic manner, tells us must be maintained. It is true, that nature can accommodate herself to the vicissitudes of heat and cold to a limited extent—as by necessity; but when wantonly persisted in, evil consequences, either immediately or remotely, will most assuredly follow.

It is of the highest importance that due attention should be paid to the senses of hearing and seeing. The first must be scrupulously guarded against excess of sounds, and the second against excess of light. These organs, especially the latter, easily become diseased by subjecting them to deep impressions. The babe should, therefore, not be taken to the window, or be exposed to the direct rays of a lamp or gas flame. This is too frequently done in order to exhibit the babe to visitors. Heat is, also, injurious to the eyes, hence the infant should not be exposed to the direct rays of a fire. These facts make it quite obvious, that the chamber should be kept quiet and dark. The two remaining senses are those of smell and taste. The infant should not inhale strong vapors. There is an instance recorded of an infant *dying from the effects of inhaling the vapors of a lininent* that was being used in the room. The infant should not, therefore, be permitted to inhale strong vapors, as camphor, ammonia, alcohol, and cologne, neither offensive odors. For this reason, soiled napkins should be promptly removed; and there should be daily changes of clothing. The sense of taste should be gratified only by the mother's breast.

Having disposed of the senses, we will now consider the instinctive desires, and reflex action of the nervous system. It is by these that the organism is excited to the exercise of its physiological functions, breathing, sucking, defecating, and urinating. To breathe is the first instinctive desire of the newly-born. There are several important conditions essential to perfect breathing. First, there must be a free supply of air, and it must be pure. An impure atmosphere is more deleterious to the young, than to those more advanced in age; and when the newly-born is struggling for existence against the adverse circumstances attending its birth, it is still more important that the air should be pure. It is at this time that the nerve centres require the stimulus of wholesome air, that the organism may not only be set in motion, but that it may continue in the healthy performance of its functions. The importance of pure air in the lying-in chamber will be more apparent, when we consider the remarkable mortality which prevailed among the infants in the Dublin lying-in hospital; and which ceased upon the adoption of Dr. Clark's suggestion, to VENTILATE THE WARDS AND ADMIT FRESH AIR THROUGHOUT THE BUILDING. Prior to the adoption of this suggestion, and during the year seventeen hundred and eighty-two, there were born in this institution, *seven thousand, six hundred and fifty* infants, of whom TWO THOUSAND, NINE HUNDRED AND FORTY-FOUR PERISHED in a manner similar to that of *carbonic acid poisoning*, which will be described presently; *third*, the expansion of the chest, and the admittance of the air into the lung-cells, completes that part of the breathing process, called *inhalation*. The inhaled air meets a supply of blood brought by the pulmonary artery from the heart into the lungs.

The blood takes up the oxygen gas and throws off the the carbonic acid gas, which is exhaled through the bronchial tubes — this process is called *exhalation.*

In the event of the blood failing to obtain a passage to the lungs, the carbonic acid will not be exhaled or eliminated from the system, where it will acumulate and act as a narcotic poison to the brain; and fatal results will necessarily follow, unless the little sufferer finds speedy succor. The indications that manifest the failing of the blood to arrive in the lungs are as follow: First, there will be observed a slight purplish hue in the complexion, particularly about the nose, lips, and nails, attended with drowsiness and languor. The purplish hue will gradually deepen, and the drowsiness grow to unconsciousness, followed by convulsions at short intervals, with increasing duration, until they become one continuous convulsion, gradually fading away with the infant's waning strength—death closing the scene. To this, the writer has frequently been a painful witness, in consequence of his being called too late to render effective aid; but he has seen these patients, by the institution of proper measures for their relief, drawn from death's tightest grasp.

Let us inquire into the cause of this failing of the blood to arrive in the lungs, and the means of its relief.

There are four cavities in the heart, two auricles and two ventricles.* The former are placed above the latter, with which they communicate by valvular openings. The auricles are separated by the auricular septum, and the

---

*R. A., right auricle; L. A., left auricle; R. V., right ventricle; L. V., left ventricle; A S., auricular septum; V. S., ventricular septum; F. O., foramen ovale; V., valve. The other valves show the direction—when the foramen ovale is closed by its valve after birth—in which the blood is to flow when both auricles simultaneously contract.

ventricles, by the ventricular septum. The right auricle receives the blood from the lungs; and the left auricle receives the blood from the systemic circulation, when the blood is thus received by the auricles, they simultaneously contract, forcing the blood into their respective ventricles. The ventricles receive the blood; and by their contraction, force it in two directions. That from the *right* ventricle—passes into the *left* ventricle—passes, through the *aorta*, into the systemic or general circulation. This is *not*, however, the case before birth. There is an opening in the auricular septum— *foramen ovale*—through which the blood passes from the *right* into the *left auricle*, as will be seen by the open valve, V, in auricular septum, as shown in the drawing, instead of the left ventricle, as above described. The opening or *foramen ovale* is *guarded* by a *valve* upon the left side of the *auricular septum*, so that when the auricles contract, the foramen is completely closed, thereby, preventing the return of the blood into the *right* auricle, and thence into the *right* ventricle; but forces the blood into the *left ventricle*, so that when this ventricle contracts, the blood will be sent coursing through the systemic or general circulation, and not into the lungs, as the fœtus can not, as yet, obtain an atmosphere to breathe. After birth, the valve over the *foramen ovale* must close and remain closed, that the blood may find its way into the *right* ventricle, and thence into the lungs. The non-performance of this act is the cause of the evil results above described. The only remedy is, to close this valve. This is accomplished by placing the infant on its *right side, with the head and shoulders well elevated.** In this position of the babe, a small

---

* The author usually advises the nurse to keep the infant in this position for a few days, as a precautionary measure; and, like advice he has tendered, upon other subjects, has been regarded only as a superstitious or foolish idea, like tying up a lock of hair on the crown of the head to keep the palate up,

quantity of blood upon the upper surface of the valve will cause it to close and keep it closed. The want of this functional performance occurs within the first week; or, the valve may become detached. This, usually, occurs within the first month or two. The writer saw an occurrence of this kind in a child a year old; and there are instances recorded of this taking place in adult life; but these are of rare occurrence.

After birth, the respiratory function marks an independent existence, and introduces a new source of heat, which, in co-operation with other processes of the economy, maintain the desired equilibrium. In consequence of the feeble exercise of the vital forces in the tender infant, the amount of heat from this new source is not sufficient with ordinary wrappings to protect it from chilling influences; but it should be so protected as to be beyond the possibility of becoming chilled.

ABLUTION OF THE NEWLY-BORN.

This should be accomplished by spreading the contents of an egg over the entire body, and then place the infant in a warm bath, where it should be well and quickly cleansed, particularly the *eyes*. Soap should not be used about the head and face, lest it should get into the eyes, to which cause grave cases of opthalmia have been traced. Then let it be quickly dried with a soft cloth, and dusted with a drying powder, such as a mixture of three parts of well-powdered starch and one part of French chalk. The belly-band is now to be well adjusted, the infant to be dressed in soft flannel, and placed in the position as above directed, and on a bed—not in a chair, to perish by some kindly visitor sitting upon, as she may think, a little *cushion*. The infant will now repose for a few hours, or until the mother shall have had some refreshment from rest and food. The infant is now ready for its first meal.

Inhuman is the mother who does not remember, with pleasing emotions, the first time she pressed the darling babe to her breast and felt its little mouth draw from her its nourishing fluid. Equally inhuman is she who is not saddened at the grievous moment when her babe "*would not take the breast*," but, by the unfeeling hand of death, passed from her. Thus it is that a benign Creator has made it incumbent upon the mother to suckle her babe; and as the obligation of protecting the offspring begins with conception, so the obligation of the mother to suckle her babe begins with its birth. Of this end the Creator has not been unmindful, but has supplied another indication of his loving kindness —the neglect of which is not unlikely to be attended with just and severe retributive evils.

The babe being now ready for its first meal, and the mother ready to serve it, they may both be placed in what may be called *the nursing posture*, *i. e.*, the mother lying upon her *left* side, the babe upon its *right*, with its head and shoulders as highly elevated as is consistent with convenience. The nipple is repeatedly placed in the infant's mouth until it "takes the breast." It draws therefrom a yellowish fluid, called *colostrum*, which is marked by characteristic effects upon the infant very different from those of the secretion when in its later stage. It is destined to meet certain exigencies, that neither milk nor any other substance can approximate in efficiency. And yet, we have daily manifestations of a disposition to turn aside from wisdom, resulting from experience and practical observation. The babe is thus victimized from the very hour of its birth, by extraneous feeding. And with what? Cow's milk, molasses, and fat bacon, are among the many pernicious things that find their way into the diet list of the newly-born! This being only one of the crude ideas of hygienic management of the young, is it at all surprising that there should be so much sickness and mortality among infants and children?

Colostrum is a nutritious fluid, and eminently appropriate to the necessities of the babe, until the "*milk comes*" It is a bland, yellowish emulsion, that dilates the stomach and purges the bowels, without producing colic and griping pains. The discharges, at first, consists of a blackish-green mucous secretion, called meconium. Unless this be discharged, it will produce serious derangements that, in some cases, have proved fatal; and, the necessity of the bowels acting at an early period is well known to mothers and nurses. When the infant is deprived of the advantages of the colostrum which nature has provided, and is fed with other articles of diet, the bowels do not act so kindly and efficiently. This is especially the case when cow's milk is substituted for nature's provision; and as it contains more cheese than mother's milk, which coagulates and clogs up the intestines, and throws the infant into convulsions; and should it escape the convulsions, the infant must then be subjected to the effects of a dose of *oil*, which is almost, if not quite, enough to terminate its existence.

The yellow granulated corpuscles of the colostrum, to which the peculiar color of the fluid is due, as well as to the sparsity of cheese and milk globules, begin to disappear on the second day, when the two latter constituents begin to increase in quantity. Thus, we have first, *yellow* milk, and then, *white* milk. The disappearance of the *corpuscles* is a very highly important circumstance; they have fulfilled their mission and must cease; their continuance induces excessive purgation, which causes the body to waste away; this affection is known as *colostration*. Whenever such symptoms appear, the mother's milk should be examined with the microscope, and if the colostrum corpuscles should be found in the milk, the infant should at once be taken from her breast, and observe the directions for feeding the infant, given hereafter.

Deep mental emotion agitating the nervous system, functional derangements of the digestive organs, and other circumstances, often cause the milk to be highly deleterious to the infant. A variety of disorders come from this source, and the mother is deprived of the pleasure of discharging one of the most important obligations due her offspring. Still more deplorable is it for the babe to have its mother wrapped in the winding sheets of death. These unfortunate circumstances render it necessary to feed the infant. But, with what?

The Apostle Paul manifested a high appreciation of the proper food of the young—"and are become such as have need of milk, and not of strong meat." The word strong may well be applied to milk, as well as meat, for as it is presented by nature in various species of animals, it differs in the strength of its various constituents to meet the necessities of the young of each species for which it was primarily intended. And we cannot feed the young of each species successfully with the milk of another, to do this, would be a violation of natural law, and the production of disastrous results. In the preparation of nourishment for the infant, let us imitate the beautiful workings of nature, by taking a half-pint of fresh milk of the cow, add half-pint water, and the cream of a second half-pint of milk, and sweeten with pure white sugar, and put it, while warm, into a bottle and cover with a gum nipple, we thus maintain the quantity of oily matter and sugar, and reduce the quantity of cheese to approximate the proportion contained in mother's milk. The *colostrum corpuscles* not being obtainable otherwise than by nature, the babe must not be deprived of their benificial effects. Should the meconium not be prompt in passing in sufficient quantity, half a grain of calomel repeated, if necessary, every five hours will be found the best course to pursue.

Having disposed of the three most important and immediate necessities of the newly-born, we will consider some of the physiological changes that transpire in the mother during gestation, and those that present themselves after the birth of the babe. The unimpregnated womb is about as large as a medium sized pear, and somewhat like it in shape. It has very thick walls, as compared with the size of its cavity. When the creative power determines there shall be another living soul, nature applies herself with diligence and exactitude to the preparation of the uterine cavity for the reception of the *primordial germ*, which is to pass from the ovary through the fallopian tube. The germ is in the prepared matrix, where it very early begins to present the form of the parent in miniature.

In the short space of nine months, the uterus increases to twelve inches in length, ten in breadth, and eight in thickness. While these rapid growths are not unattended with their requisite drafts, and disturbing effects upon the mother's economy, there are also evidences of provision being made for the nutrition of the fœtus; and, also, prospectively, for the sustenance of the infant after birth. Hence, immediately following impregnation, and increase in the size of the uterus, there are two sets of physiological changes that manifest themselves.

First.—The digestive processes of the mother begin to elaborate, and place in her blood the various elements of the requisite *pabulum* for the development and sustenance of the offspring. These consist of butter, albumen, cheese, earthy phosphates, and iron. When these constituents are in superabundance, they are eliminated by some of the emunctories. For this reason, the urine of the pregnant female frequently contains albumen, the simples of all animal products; also, a substance called *kiestine*, which, perhaps, is the intermediate state in the metamorphosis of albumen into cheese. The non-elimination of the surplus of these albuminous compounds from the system is among the causes of the nervous derangements and diseases that accompany pregnancy, or attend the female in her confinement.

Second.—This set of physiological changes relate to the breasts. By these, the elaborated food is separated from the blood and given to the infant. To this end, they take upon themselves increased nutrition, which is shown by their increased size, firmness, enlarged veins, coloration of the areola, prominence of the nipples, and *finally*, a watery discharge upon drawing the breasts; *the colostrum*, described above as *yellow milk*, and very soon passes into *white milk*, which now requires special attention.

4

WHITE MILK.

This is the food for the young of animals and of man. In the growth and development of the fabric, it supplies:

a. The cheese or caseine. This substance is held in solution by the milk when fresh, and is distinguished from the other proteine compounds by its containing no phosphorus. In the construction of the soft parts, such as the skin, muscle, lung, liver, kidney, brain, and nerve, it supplies the carbon, hydrogen, oxygen, and nitrogen, which are the ultimate chemical constituents of these tissues.

b. The frame-work to support and build the flesh upon is next to be considered. It consists of bone, which is formed of the phosphatic salts of lime, soda, potassa, and magnesia, held together by *glue* (bone glue), another one of the proteine compounds of animal matter. When there is an insufficient supply of these salts, the frame-work will be soft and flexible, producing a variety of deformitives. These salts are found in healthy, natural mother's milk in great abundance.

c. We have already noticed the importance of heat in the developing processes, and in the maintenance of a healthy state of the human economy. To this end, there is a most ample provision found in mother's milk; and consists in the sugar, one of the *carbohydrates*, a class of substances, which are found almost exclusively in the vegetable kingdom, and are made up of carbon, hydrogen, and oxygen. The nitrogen is omitted in this class, which is the distinction between formative and respiratory food. Thus, we have a supply of carbon to unite with the oxygen brought by the air inhaled into the lungs, and of oxygen to unite with the carbon which may be set free in the changes which are constantly taking place throughout the entire body, by which heat is produced, the temperature of which is regulated by physiological forces to be hereafter considered.

d. The brain and nerves find an ample supply of phosphorus (in combination with the lime, soda, and potassa) in mothers' milk. This is an essential element in their construction, and for the full performance of their functions.

e. All chemical and vital formative processes require water for the solution of the elementary constituents which enter into the formation of the newly developed substance, and for which purpose water is supplied by the milk. Thus, efficiently, wonderfully, and wisely, mother's milk meets all the requisites of the offspring. This fluid is supplied by the mammary glands of the mother; and the physiologist studies the many formations of tissue to which milk is so well adapted; but the interesting glandular structures by which the milk is separated from the blood and conveyed to the infant, are equally attractive of his admiration. He can not but appreciate the importance of their continued healthy state to meet the performance of their secretive functions; and the whole period of pregnancy, attended with a constantly increasing efflux of blood to these glands, is a preparatory stage to this end. God thus plainly shows that, the proper nutriment of the babe is its mother's milk. When the infant is nourished by other means than the breast, the nursing instincts are lost; the breasts are imperfectly drawn, the congestion increases, the cheese coagulates within the ducts, mammary abcess follows, and, perhaps, a loss of the utility of the glands as a sad result.

In the healthy and well-formed infant there is usually no difficulty in getting the bowels and the bladder to discharge their contents. Should, however, these organs fail to perform their functions in due time, the parts must be examined for any malformation that might exist; and if there should be any discovered, the infant must be put into the hands of a competent surgeon. If the parts are found to be properly formed, then recourse must be had to remedial agents.

The infant being born, and its immediate necessities supplied, its organism is so feeble through, at least, the first month as to cause it to spend almost the whole time in sleep —occasionally awaking to take its meals. This tendency to sleep is no more a special provision of nature for the infant than for the adult. The former sleeps for the want of strength of the vital forces to maintain the wakeful state; and the latter sleeps to restore the exhausted strength of the vital forces. Sleep is of the utmost importance to the infant, and should be duly managed. The position in which the infant should be placed during the hours of repose until it is, at least, a week old, has already been described. After this time, the babe may be placed on its back or either side. The objection to the former is, that the spittle is apt to trickle into the air passages and strangle the infant. It is advisable to change the position occasionally, as the babe has not the strength to relieve itself of an uncomfortable or even a painful posture, and of the cause and manner of relief it is even unconscious. The infant should sleep with the mother; but much care should be exercised in regard to its relation to her and the bedding. The weight of the covering should not be such as to press heavily upon the infant; neither should it be permitted to slip down under the bedclothes in such a manner as to cause it to inhale an atmosphere contaminated with the effluvia from the body of the mother. More than this, the infant is liable to be smothered, instances of which have frequently occurred. After the first month, the infant may, in hot seasons of the year, sleep in the cradle, both night and day; but in cold weather the babe should, invariably, be the bed-companion of the mother. The cradle is a convenient piece of furniture, and, notwithstanding the opposition it meets with, it still retains its place in the nursery. When the babe is laid upon the bed, it is apt to roll off, or garments are apt to be thrown upon, and either injure or smother it; or, if it sleeps upon a lounge, it is liable to be sat upon by some careless visitor. The infant is secured against these accidents by placing it in a cradle or crib. In addition to this, by the portability of the crib, the babe can be placed in any convenient place in the room. In cold weather, it should be near the fire, and never in a current of air, or near a window or door, where the cold air will fall upon the sleeper. When the sheets are wet with urine, the nurse must not content herself by drying them, but they should be changed; and this rule should be observed in regard to the napkins and skirts of the infant; and in making these changes, the newly-washed should be exposed to the fire, that perfect dryness may be insured. By the observance of this rule, the babe will never be put to bed with damp wrappings, thus avoiding this cause of disease. In the early periods of infancy, after feeding, the babe will fall into a state of repose; whereas, when older, it will be necessary to "put the babe to sleep." Some people, to avoid the loss of time and trouble, place the infant in a cradle, and tell it, "Now go to sleep." This seems harsh and unmotherly, and is not the treatment the infant expects to receive from the parent. But rather let the sleep steal over the closing eyes under the influence of a lullaby song.

It is not sufficient for the infant to sleep, but the character of the sleep is of much importance. It should be calm and sweet, otherwise, it cannot be refreshing, or effective in the development of the vital forces. The sleep must be profound and undisturbed, consequently, there should be no confusion in the nursery. The necessity of sleep makes it important that it should be attended with those conditions, which favor its continuance, until the wakeful state ensues from natural causes; and never be put to sleep unless it is naturally sleepy. The infant is occasionally victimized to the convenience of the mother, or nurse, by the administration of an opiate, which is criminally wrong; and another great wrong, is to awake the infant to be bathed and dressed, at the convenience of the mother. Light, being inimical to profound sleep, should be excluded. It is better to accomplish this exclusion by use of the window curtains or shutters, than by surrounding the crib with curtains, which deprives the babe of the advantages of a free circulating atmosphere. Through the smallness of the stomach and the feebleness of the digestive organs, the infant cannot receive and digest the quantity of food necessary to sustain the organism through eight successive hours of sleep. The sleep will, therefore, cease, the respiratory muscles will become exhausted, and the infant becoming uncomfortable, will awaken hungry, and eagerly seek the mother's breast. Infants differ, however; some will sleep all night, awaking only early in the morning to take their meal, while others, again, will require the breast two to four times during the night; much of this depends upon habit. If the infant sleep much through the day, it will be more wakeful during the night; and if not put to bed until it is quite wearied and sleepy, and retires with a full meal, the sleep will be prolonged, profound, and refreshing.

PART IV.

INFANCY.

At about the end of the first month, the impressions that have been made upon the senses will have disclosed in the infant the possession of those faculties with which it enters upon its life-time of discoveries. It will gradually become familiar with those who administer to its daily wants, with surrounding objects, and with the sound of the language it is to speak. The transition of the organism, through the organic changes peculiar to this period of life, is not only interesting, but a knowledge of them is highly important to the better understanding of the proper management of the babe. It is also interesting to observe, that while the infant is undergoing the organic changes consequent upon development, its constitution is becoming adapted and moulded to the manner of its future life. The formative processes of the bones and of the soft tissues, in addition to the demands made by the usual waste of the general economy, requires a liberal supply of nutriment. Hence it is, that every part of the infant's economy is more freely supplied with blood than that of the adult. The pulsation of the heart is more frequent, it being one hundred and twenty-five to one hundred and thirty per minute. The skin is soft, tender, and sensitive. The head is proportionately larger, as is also the liver. The digestive organs feebly perform their functions, and the mucous membrane of the alimentary canal is quite sensitive—so much so that convulsions are easily induced by the presence of indigestible matter within the stomach or bowels. It is, perhaps, for the more perfect protection of this sensitive membrane that there is a thick coating of mucous spread over its surface in such manner as to give the appearance of a false membrane. The discharge of this mucous takes place, occasionally, in such quantities as will excite a suspicion of a diseased condition of the bowels, and the infant is placed under treatment for the supposed disease, when, in fact, the symptom is nothing more than one of nature's sanitary measures.

During the term of pregnancy, the fœtus is in such a compressed state, that those muscles which flex or draw up the limbs, and double the body upon itself, are in a constant state of contraction; and those which extend the limbs, and support the body in an erect posture, are necessarily drawn out to their full length. This relation of the flexor and extensor muscles obtains during our sleeping hours, especially after much physical exertion during the day, when the extensor muscles gradually relax, and the flexor muscles slowly contract, like a piece of gum-elastic when slightly drawn out and then laid upon a table; this slow contraction is occasionally attended with a spasmodic action, by which the sleeper is started, and sometimes awakened from his slumbers; and when we arise from our night's repose, we must *pandiculate* or *stretch*, in order to restore the equipoise of these two sets of muscles. This uneven state of the muscles is persistent long after birth, and exercise is necessary to equipoise them, so that the infant can extend the arm, as in reaching forth for an object; to extend the leg, as in walking; and to keep the body erect, as in standing.

By proper management, the muscular system will be sufficiently equipoised and developed, at the expiration of twelve months, to enable the babe to walk, and to present a beautiful and graceful figure; whereas, if improperly managed, the infant will be sluggish in its movements, and present an ungraceful appearance—if not absolutely deformed. In the early months of infancy, the exercise must necessarily be passive, and this will be afforded by the handling to which the infant is subjected in its nursings, dressings, and ablutions, as well as by the voluntary movements of its extremities.

It is highly important that the babe should be handled with the utmost gentleness and care. The necessity of this is made more patent by an appreciation of the feebleness of its organism. The bones are soft, loosely and feebly connected with each other. The muscles are too small and feeble to support the head and to keep the spine erect. It is through the feebleness of the muscles that the infant's head falls helplessly upon its shoulders, and that the spine curves upon itself unless otherwise supported. For these reasons, it is highly reprehensible to *toss* or *throw the infant* up and down or dandle it upon the knee. Infants are occasionally subjected to such violent treatment, either to amuse them or to quiet their cries—when it is neither amusing nor any relief to their sufferings. On the contrary, it augments their sufferings, and may become the exciting cause of disease and deformities. Instead of such rough handling—the carrying of the infant constantly in the arms of the nurse, whereby its extremities are restricted in their movements—common sense would dictate the cradle or the floor as the place, and its clothing being so arranged as to permit free motion of its extremities. It is by the instinctive throwing about of its arms and legs that its muscles become evenly developed.

Infants delight in the open air and sunshine, in riding in the baby carriage, drawn over a smooth pathway; while the inhalation of fresh air, the warmth of genial sunbeams, the change of scenery combined with exercise, add greatly to the healthy development of both body and mind. Therefore, the infant should be taken into the open air as often as the state of the weather will admit—remembering, however, that exposure to an atmosphere of low temperature, without sufficient wrappings, will bring about *catarrhal fever*, bronchitis, and pneumonia; and that exposure to a damp atmosphere is an efficient cause of rheumatic affections. These diseases are also brought about by exposure to draughts of wind, and those draughts or currents are formed by the streets. Thus it is that the idle habit of "*standing on the corner*" is productive of "*bad colds.*" When the nurse takes the babe into the streets for an airing, she should be instructed *not* to stand on the corner, and to *keep on the lee side of the buildings.* In complying with these instructions, the infant may be saved from sickness, and perhaps death. However, when the weather is inclement, it is far better that the babe should be within doors. It is quite refreshing to the babe to be taken from one apartment to another, and to be shown objects it has not recently seen. When taken in the arms of another, the nurse or attendant should enforce the proper manner in which it should be carried. The infant should be carried alternately upon each arm, that the pressure may be equalized, and thereby preventing any deformity that might arise from this cause: as, when the babe is carried constantly upon the same arm, one side would grow, and the other be stunted. Because of the softness of the spine, the body of the infant must be supported by the shoulder and hands, while the extremities are left unrestrained.

The infant should not be permitted to bear its entire weight upon its legs until it is at least nine or ten months old. At this age, it will begin to climb up by a chair, then to stand alone, and then to walk. The infant will occasionally get a fall, and a little fright, by which it will learn there is danger in falling. Without the trials and mishaps of early life, the child would grow up timid and irresolute. Infants who are not afforded nurses are more resolute and self-reliant, and require less attention, than those who are constantly under the supervision of an attendant.

Of the many processes of infantile development, that of dentition brings with it the greatest anxiety, because of its painfulness, and of the danger of its becoming the exciting cause of grave complications and general derangements of the whole economy. There are none that should invite our closer attention, and lead us to more careful provision against its perils. Dentition is a normal process, and is governed by natural laws; hence, well-developed and healthy infants, and those free from hereditary diseases, will pass its periods with little inconvenience or suffering. But those of feeble organizations, and those affected by hereditary ailments are apt, through teething, to fall victims to disease. It is both interesting and important to know the history of teeth formation; but only an outline of the process is allowed by the limits of this work. At the sixth and seventh week of intra-uterine existence, the mucous membrane of the jaw-bone forms a groove along the edge of the maxillary arch, where the teeth are to appear. A papilla for each tooth is then formed in this groove, which is called the papillary stage. The groove is developed into a follicle, which finally closes the papillæ. This is the second, or follicular, stage. The papillæ begin to grow quite rapidly. At about the thirteenth week they become pulpy, and receive the forms of the future teeth. At the fifth month of fœtal existence, the dentine begins to form upon the pulp of the teeth, preparatory to the

ERUPTION OF THE DECIDUOUS, TEMPORARY, OR MILK TEETH.

These are twenty in number, of which EIGHT are *incisors*, FOUR *canine*, and EIGHT *molars*. The incisors are so named from their presenting a sharp edge for cutting the food, and situated in front of the mouth, four in each jaw, two central, and two lateral. The *canine teeth*, from *canis*, a *dog*, are also called *cuspidati*, from *cuspido*, to point or make sharp at the end. There are two in each jaw, one placed behind each lateral incisor. Those in the upper jaw are commonly called *eye-teeth*, and those in the lower jaw, *stomach teeth*. The *molars*, or grinders, so called from the Latin *mola*, a mill, number four in each jaw, two being placed behind each of the *canine* teeth. These are distinguished as the first and second, or anterior and posterior molars.

DENTITION.

Dentitio (the breeding or cutting of teeth), begins and proceeds in the following order, viz.:

Sixth to seventh month, central incisors.
Seventh to tenth month, lateral incisors.
Twelfth to fourteenth month, anterior molars.
Fourteenth to twentieth month, canine.
Eighteenth to thirty-sixth month, posterior molars.

Instances of great deviations from the above periods of eruption occasionally occur. When there is a premature development of the bones, dentition will also take place earlier than usual; while, on the other hand, in cases of slowness of bone formation, dentition is apt to meet with a corresponding delay. When these latter conditions obtain, especially when associated with a puny or an unhealthy state, the infant should be placed under treatment. In such cases, the administration of the hypophosphates is of great advantage.

The deciduous or temporary teeth subserve the purpose of mastication until the sixth or seventh year, by which time the roots are absorbed by the pressure of the permanent teeth, which now begin to develop, and become complete about the twentieth year. The process of eruption of the deciduous teeth is divisible into two stages, viz.:

The first consists in an expansion of the capsule and its pressing against the gum, which gives rise to an unpleasant or itching sensation, and relief is obtained by counter-pressure, or rubbing the gum. Hence, the babe will, almost constantly, have its fingers in its mouth, and will carry there everything it can grasp, with a view of relieving itself of the uneasiness. The irritation will extend to other parts of the mouth, and the effect upon the salivary glands is manifested by an increased flow of saliva, which, heretofore, was quite inconsiderable. As the expansion of the capsule progresses, the irritation will extend to other parts, until the general economy is affected. The infant now becomes restless. It will cry at one moment, and laugh the next. These two expressions of opposite emotions will become so intermingled that it will often be difficult to distinguish between them. Twitchings and wakefulness disturb the sleep. The appetite becomes impaired, and the bowels relaxed. The infant is much relieved of these disturbances by incising the gum, although the tooth may not appear above the gum for several weeks. This stage terminates by a cessation of all indications of teething, and the constitutional disturbances will lull for a month or six weeks, to be again excited by the

Second stage: This commences by the renewal of the above symptoms in a more aggravated form. The tooth now rises out of the capsule, and pierces the strong fibrous tissue of the gum, which becomes much harder, and under the lancet imparts a sensation similar to that of cutting sole-leather. The arrest of the circulation in the gum from the pressure of the tooth, gives the gum a blanched appearance, and this, combined with its hardness, makes the gum have somewhat the appearance of true cartilage. When the tooth is well advanced, the gum becomes relaxed, the circulation returns, a red spot forms at the place where the tooth is to appear, and then the gums become swollen and tender. Relief is no longer obtained by pressure, or by rubbing the gum; on the contrary, such treatment is quite painful; hence, the babe will not put its fingers into the mouth, nor permit the gums to be touched. The irritability increases; the babe will take its toys and immediately throw them aside. Even the breast is only taken to be rejected. Neither is the babe quiet in any position in which it may be placed. There is a constant irritable fretfulness, which is extremely wearying to the attendant. Although such is the ordinary course of a well-marked case of teething, yet cases occur in which every degree of inconvenience and suffering is experienced, from those who pass through the stages, without attracting the attention of the parents or attendants until the tooth is discovered to be through the gum—to those who succumb to the complications of difficult dentition. There is also a difference in the degree of suffering consequent upon the eruption of the several teeth. The *central incisors* are quite easy in their eruption, while the *lateral incisors* occasion more suffering, and the *molars* rather less than the latter. The canine are usually attended with the greatest difficulty, and their process of eruption during the hot months is the cause of the infant suffering through its second summer.

    The most natural inquiry that arises in the mind of the parent is: Are there any means by which the sufferings and perils of dentition may be averted? Happily, observation, experience, and science reply: There are, and they may be employed with much efficacy. A happy issue out of the teething periods is much dependent upon the quality of the food the infant eats, of the air it breathes, and the manner of its dressing, previous to the beginning of the eruptive processes.

OF THE FOOD.

The natural source of nourishment for the newly-born has already been considered—the mother's breasts. And there is no kind of food which is so well adapted to the wants of the constitution, and none so agreeable to the taste of the infant, until the appearance of the deciduous teeth, as mother's milk. These two facts become more patent when it is considered that the peculiarities of the constitution and of the blood of the mother are transmitted to the infant, by which a natural correlation is established between the mother and her offspring, which is strengthened by habit and co-adaptation, to a degree that cannot obtain between the babe and another woman. Thus, in compliance with physiological law, as well as natural love and regard for the welfare of the offspring, it not only becomes the duty of the mother to suckle her babe, but also to supply a sufficient quantity of good milk. And in order that this end may be attained, the mother must be instructed as to the regimen best suited to the nursing female. This information, however, would be of little advantage to the infant, unless the mother should cheerfully comply with all that the regimen may demand.

Reference has already been made to the several constituents of a normal secretion from the mammary glands of the nursing female, and the part they perform in the nutritive processes of the offspring. But a knowledge of their physical and chemical properties is not only essential to the proper management of the mother through the nursing period; but also for the proper treatment of the babe. When the milk is fresh from the mother's breast, it is a white, opaque, sweet, and slightly alkaline fluid, consisting of water, holding in solution salines, sugar, and caseine, with a quantity of oleaginous matter, and butter suspended in an emulsified or milk-like form; and when taken into the infant's stomach, it is easy of digestion and highly nutritious, without disturbing the economy by nausea and vomiting, purging and griping pains. Its efficacy as a nutriment for the babe cannot be equalled by any other fluid or article of diet that art can produce. The salines consist of phosphate of iron, soda, lime, potassa, and magnesia, with a trace of chloride of sodium and of potassium. The salines are derived from the blood of the mother, and are nearly identical with the salts of that fluid; and as the quantity is proportionally greater in the milk, *springs* and *wells* should, therefore, supply the nursing mother with the water by which she slakes her thirst, and *not* cisterns, into which water is gathered from eaves-drippings; for such water does not contain those salts which, as we have seen, is so *essential* to the *young*. So long as the milk retains its alkaline reaction, the caseine is held in solution; but when the milk becomes sour, the caseine is precipitated. This change in the milk necessarily takes place in the stomach, as the first step in the digestive process; and when the infant has taken large quantities of milk into its stomach, or when the digestive organs have become enfeebled from some irritating cause, such as teething, flakes of coagulated cheese will appear in the ejections; whereupon, the anxious mother unnecessarily has the babe treated for diseased bowels. The proper course, however, is to let the babe alone, unless there should be some general disturbance. Then the babe should be restrained from nursing too freely; and should the disturbance continue, an aperient, such as half a grain of calomel, or a teaspoonful of spiced syrup of rhubarb, should be administered. The caseine of mother's milk is not so readily precipitated upon the addition of acids as that of cow's milk; from which it may be inferred that the former is more soluble than the latter. This difference between the two kinds of caseine is in favor of mother's milk, and strongly supports the opinion of its better adaptation to the digestive organs of the infant than the milk of the cow.

The milk-globules consist of a peculiar fatty substance, known as butter, and is composed of glycerine, united with various acids, which form butyrate, capronate, caprate, and oleate of glycerine. The first of these is the one to which the odor of butter is due. Milk sugar, found only in animal milk, supplies the babe with the carbon which, in its conversion into carbonic acid by the inhaled oxygen of the air, aids in producing and maintaining the necessary temperature of the body. We have already seen that the milk which is secreted immediately after delivery, is widely different, both in its properties and in its constituents, from that which is secreted a few days after the birth of the infant. This alteration in the properties and in the constituents of the milk, is attended with a gradual increase of the salines and of the caseine, to meet the increased demands of the infant. These two constituents continue to increase until about the second month, after which time any change in their proportional quantities will depend upon the diet of the mother, and the state of her health. The oil-globules attain to their maximum quantity within the first month. After this time, the relative proportion of milk-globules will depend upon the quantity of fatty matter which enters into the mother's diet. It also appears from analysis that the sugar attains to its maximum quantity within the first month, and that each succeeding month, until the sixth, the milk has less and less sugar.

It is of the highest degree of importance to the healthy development of the infant, for the milk to be secreted in sufficient quantity and of good quality. As regards the first of these, the quantity secreted in a given length of time cannot be definitely ascertained, because the infant can draw a larger quantity of milk from the breast than can be drawn with fingers or a breast-pump. A knowledge of the exact amount of milk secreted in a given length of time is, however, of little practical importance, inasmuch as infants differ in the amount of food required for their sustenance and growth; and the quantity for the nourishment of the infant also depends upon the exact degree of the richness of the milk in its various constituents. Therefore, the question is not, How much milk is secreted? but rather, Does the babe obtain a sufficient amount of nourishment from the mother's breast? As the infant cannot express itself vocally, we must learn to interpret the manner of expression peculiar to them; and there is nothing which will elicit from an infant stronger manifestations of displeasure than an insufficient supply of milk to fill its stomach, for the infant does not crave the breast so much to satisfy hunger, as to fill the stomach; and when it accomplishes this, it is quite satisfied; and when this organ is emptied, either by the digestive process, or by regurgitation, it will again demand the breast.

And when the quantity of milk obtained is insufficient to fill the stomach, the infant will fret at the breast; and it now becomes a difficult task, indeed, to divert its mind from the partially-filled stomach. How differently it will behave when the supply is adequate to its wants! It will quit its meal fully satisfied, and will fall asleep, or return to its amusing frolics, without exhausting the supply in the breast.

We will consider only a few of the causes of a diminished flow of the secretion. Cases in which the breasts are insufficiently developed are of rare occurrence. But when this occurs, we then have an example of the promptness with which nature responds to calls when made upon her, for when the infant is put to the breasts, they will increase in size until they are sufficient to secrete the quantity of milk adequate to the wants of the infant. The excitement of the nutritive nerves of the mammary glands, caused by the infant sucking the nipple, is not only helpful to their farther development, but it is also the most potent means of inducing a flow of the secretion. Even men have been enabled to act as wet-nurses, by the frequent application of the infant to the breasts. An opposite condition is sometimes met with—in enlargement of the glands. This enlargement of the glands may be due to an increase in size of the glandular structure itself, or to an accumulation of fat about it. This deposition of fat presents no impediment to the act of nursing, nor to the infant obtaining an adequate quantity of milk. The nipple is sometimes so contracted as to prevent the infant from grasping it with the mouth. Such contracted nipples can be drawn out with a breast-pump, a nipple-glass, or by taking a vial with a mouth sufficiently large, immerse it in boiling water for a few moments, and then, when empty and the rim of the mouth is cooled a little, by dipping in cold water, apply to the nipple and press a small wet cloth over the vial, which, upon cooling, will draw the nipple out sufficiently for the infant to draw. The author has frequently resorted to this little expedient with perfect success. A more painful and annoying complication of the breast, is an inflammatory action, terminating in *mammary abscess.* While this complication is met with in any period in the course of lactation, it most usually occurs shortly after the "milk comes" or when the caseine and milk globules appear in increased quantity. There is no disease more tractable than mammery abscess in the lying-in female; provided the treatment be commenced sufficiently early, properly conducted, and, above all, the patient *be properly nursed.* Among the most efficient remedies for this affection is, fluid ext. poke. Twenty drops to be given every three hours until relief is obtained. The writer has had many occasions to be grateful for an agent so efficient as this one article.

In further consideration of the mammary glands, we find there are conditions of other organs of the economy, which lessen the quantity of the secretion; but a full account of them would be too extensive for our present purpose. Among the most important, however, are the following, viz.: Intense and often repeated mental emotion, acute inflammatory disease, dyspepsia, pregnancy, and a return of the menstrual discharge, and issues of whatever kind. All these will affect the quantity and quality of the milk, and in a sad degree disqualifies the mother to act as a nurse for her babe.

Agalaxy. This word implies either, a deficiency supply, or an absence of the milk; and a *galactagogue*, is a medicine, or an agent, by which the glands are excited to the performance of their secreting function. The application of the infant to the breast has already been mentioned as a potent means of inducing a flow of milk.* M. Becquerel used electricity as a *gælactagogue*; and succeeded in restoring the secretion after a total suspension in one of the glands, while there was but little remaining in the other. The inhabitants of Cape de Verde Islands, highly esteem the castor oil plant for this purpose. The plant is used by making a strong decoction of the leaves, with which the breasts are bathed for a short time, and then some of the leaves are laid upon the breasts, and permitted to remain until they become dry. It is said, there are two varieties of this plant: viz.—white and red. The natives use the former, and regard the latter as possessing no galactagogue milk-producing virtues whatever.

The milk as supplied by the mother's breasts may be sufficient in quantity, to fill the stomach of the nursling; and yet, be insufficient to nourish the general economy, and then the infant is said—*"not to thrive at the breast."* So long as the nourishing fluid is sufficient to meet the immediate necessities of the infant, i. e., to fill its stomach, it will no longer express itself in the manner as above described, although the milk may be deficient in its inherent properties, and the infant suffering the consequences. The effects of this latter condition of the milk upon the infant will be such as are produced by a slow process of *inanition* or *starvation*. These effects will steal so slowly upon the little sufferer as to pass unnoticed until the more marked results ensue, such as extreme emaciation, diarrhœa, or an eruption upon the cutaneous surface.

*See Braithwait Retrosp. Part 36.

And for these supposed *acute* diseases, the mother obtains professional advice; whereupon the case is learnedly named and classified, and the poor sufferer is victimized to dosings of cod-liver oil with whiskey, astringents, alteratives, and tonics; whilst the true nature and cause of the afflictions are wholly lost sight of by both mother and physician, and the infant *dies*.

Under this slow process of starvation, the brain does not receive its due stimulus, and the nervous system is not sustained. The subject, therefore, becomes less animate and displays less energy in its frolics. The sleep becomes less refreshing and more disturbed. The fat now ceases to increase in quantity, and then begins to be absorbed to supply the deficiency of combustive material in the nourishing fluid obtained from the mother. Anorexia or loss of appetite sets in. The organs cease to perform, with due regularity, their daily functions. The effete matters, which, as we have already seen, are incompatible with a continued healthy state of the economy, now remain in the system, and there supply the pabulum for the virulent growth of pestiferous diseases. This is graphically presented in the following quotation:

"A deficiency of food, especially of the nitrogenous part, quickly leads to the breaking up of the animal frame. Plague, pestilence, and famine are associated in the public mind, and the records of every country show how closely they are related. The medical history of Ireland is remarkable for the illustrations of how much mischief may be occasioned by a general deficiency of food. Always the habitat of fever, it every now and then becomes the very hot-bed of its propagation and development. Let there be but a small failure in the usually imperfect supply of food, and the lurking seeds of pestilence are ready to burst into frightful activity. The famine of the present century is but a too forcible illustration of this. It fostered epidemics which had not been witnessed in this generation, and gave rise to scenes of devastation and misery which are not surpassed by the most appalling epidemics of the Middle Ages. The principal form of the scourge was known as the contagious famine fever (typhus), and it spread, not merely from end to end of the country in which it had originated, but, breaking through all boundaries, it crossed the ocean, and made itself painfully manifest in localities where it was previously unknown. Thousands fell under the virulence of its action, for wheresoever it came, it struck down a seventh of the people, and of those whom it attacked, one out of nine perished. Even those who escaped the fatal influence of it were left the miserable victims of scurvy and low fever. Another example not less striking, of the terrible consequences of what may be truly called famine, was the condition of our troops during the early part of their sojourn in the Crimea, in 1854. With only just enough of food to maintain the integrity of the system at a time of repose, and at ordinary temperatures, they were called upon to make large muscular exertions, and to sustain the warmth of the system, in the midst of severe cold."*

The whole matter of feeding the offspring should be entrusted to the *mother*, who should be qualified by the possession of a thorough knowledge of all the practical details of feeding the young, and to be able to quickly apprehend whatever may go amiss. Such a mother will, when it becomes necessary to have professional advice, be able to place before the physician such facts as will lead him to a correct diagnosis of the case and to such treatment as will bring about a cure. The author has met with such women, and they were, in the true sense of the word, *mothers*.

There is scarcely a circumstance in the affairs of infantile existence that affords more serious grounds of regret than that the infant should be deprived of its mother's breasts as its source of nourishment. And this becomes a matter of greater moment when we consider the imperfectly developed

---

* See AITKEN, *Science and Practice of Medicine*, vol. 1, p. 737.

state of those glands which supply the secretions which are essential to the conversion of food into chyme, and then into chyle; and then the absorbents are not yet capable of performing their function in a vigorous manner. Take, for instance, the salivary glands. The secretions from these organs are of the highest importance in the digestion of certain substances, for which purpose it flows freely into the mouth and is mixed with the food during mastication. Whereas, with the infant, as we have already seen, the mouth is quite dry until the eruptive process begins, when the irritation caused by the coming teeth excites a flow of saliva preparatory to the digestion of food stronger than milk. And if we were to continue our investigations of the secretions of all the digestive organs of the infant as we have that of the salivary glands, we would not be long in arriving at the conclusion that we might as well expect a rich harvest from seed sown upon a sandy plain, as to expect the infant to *thrive* when fed upon food so unsuited to the physiology of its organism. Such articles of food consist of soups, pap, panada and gruel, made of water, flour, oat meal, corn-meal and molasses, which require for their digestion, the powers of the adult organism. What results then may we expect to accrue to the infant from such unnatural feedings, other than gastric irritation, diarrhœa, enlargement of the mesenteric glands, hepatic derangements, emaciation, jaundice, convulsions, and death? Doubtless there are mothers and nurses who will regard all this as the product of a fertile imagination; but when we review the practical results obtained from the efforts that have been made to "*bring up children by hand*," we find the above to be an appalling reality.

In institutions provided for the benefit of foundlings,

and where it is imposible to provide wet nurses for such great numbers of these little dependents, the death rate resulting from this one cause only, viz.: *the unfitness of the food to the manner in which the digestive organs perform their functions in early life*—kill from FORTY TO NINETY IN ONE HUNDRED *of those suffering infants.* Is not this alarming? Do we not learn from this a lesson sufficient to keep mothers and nurses from cramming their infants with vile amylaceous (or starchy) compounds, under the false idea that mother's milk, *alone*, is insufficient to sustain and to nourish the infantile organism?

It is true, that, in the rural districts, where the infant obtains a pure atmosphere, wholesome waters from springs and wells, pure fresh milk supplied at all times by the same cow, and the undivided attention of the mother or nurse, the mortality among children reared by hand is much less than among those who dwell in cities and especially in asylums. However great these advantages may be, all observers and authors are agreed as touching this one point, viz.: the rearing of infants by hand is attended with great risk to the health, and life itself, of the infant; and for these reasons should be conducted with the utmost care, attention and precaution.

We have already considered the necessity of providing for the unfortunate infant an article of food, possessing, as nearly as possible, all the properties belonging to mother's milk; and that this is obtained by mixing a quantity of cow's milk with its bulk of water, and the richness of cream maintained by the addition of that which is taken from a like quantity of milk, and the sweetness, by the addition of pure, white sugar. Let it be remembered, that the caseine of cow's milk is not so soluble as that of mother's milk, and as carbonate of soda exercises the power of promoting the solubility of caseine, therefore, a trace of this substance may, with great propriety, be added to the fluid. After the food is thus prepared, let it be warmed and then put in a conveniently sized bottle that is *absolutely* clean and dried in the sun or heated by the fire, and when covered with a gum nipple it is ready to be given to the infant, who, if healthy and in good condition as regards all the circumstances which constitute *comfort*, will eagerly seize the bottle and carry the nipple to its mouth, and relish a hearty meal. And let this be repeated as often as the infant asks for its meals in the language which the mother or nurse so soon learns. The healthy infant should be the sole judge as to the quantity to be taken at a meal, and that will be when its stomach is full.

Now, this whole proceeding seems, to many mothers, to be quite simple, in fact, so much so, that they will entrust the preparation of the food, and the feeding of their offspring to a careless, slip-shod servant woman, or even to a *little girl* employed in the family as a *nurse*. Were it possible for all the dead infants to arise from their graves, and tell the world what had been the prime cause of their death, the number of those who would point to the careless manner in which their food had been prepared, and the condition of their nursing bottles, would be appalling! astounding!! overwhelming!!! Therefore, *mothers, do not let your infants perish for the lack of your personal care and supervision.* For this is a duty that Nature's God imperatively imposes upon you.

The importance of exercising great care, and of taking the utmost precaution in feeding the young, are of such moment as to demand special notice.

In the preparation of the food, as above described, the first step is to obtain *fresh* cow's milk, and at all times supplied by the same cow. The mother must, if possible, and of her own knowledge, *know* these to be the real conditions of the milk. It is of equal importance for her to *know* that the milk has been properly handled. All the vessels, and strainers into, and through which the milk is to pass, should be *absolutely free* from the slightest trace of old milk adhering to any part of the vessels. This degree of cleanliness can be obtained, only by having a number of vessels sufficient to admit of daily changes, and after a thorough scalding and washing, let them lie a day exposed to the sun and air. The water should be obtained from a spring or well, that the quantity of earthy salts may be maintained in the food, whereas, if soft water is used, it is quite obvious that the proportion of these salts would be reduced to just one-half the quantity that nature has designed to be sufficient to supply the necessities of the offspring. There should be only a small quantity of the food prepared at one time. Three or more druggists' prescription vials of four or six ounces capacity, with a like number of gum nipples should be obtained, and kept constantly at hand. And the same constant care should be exercised in regard to the cleanliness of the nursing bottles and nipples as is bestowed upon the milk-vessels. As gum-tubes can not be cleansed and aired so readily and perfectly, let them be expunged from the nursery as you would poison, for doubtless they have been the prime cause of the death of many infants; and for this reason, their use in feeding children can not be condemned in language too strong. When indications of teething begin to appear, the saliva increases with the advancing teeth until the flow is quite free, which is an indication that the organism is approaching that stage of development preparatory to the digestion of food other than milk. If, however, the infant is *thriving* on the "*nursing-bottle,*" or at the breast, let well enough alone; but if in connection with the beginning of the teething process, and the increased flow of saliva, there should be any indications of the infant becoming dissatisfied with its food, or of its getting into a *bad condition*, it would be expedient to introduce a change of diet. The milk may now be less diluted with water, or, thickened with arrow-root. *Liebig's soup* is represented, by those who have had experience in its use, as being admirably suited to the wants of the infant, and is made as follows:—

Take of wheat flour and dried malt, each, one-half ounce; bicarb. potassa, seven and one-half grains; water, one ounce; mix, and add milk, five ounces. Put the vessel on a fire, and, with constant stirring, heat slowly until the mixture begins to thicken; then the vessel is to be removed from the fire, and the stirring continued for ten minutes. This process is to be repeated the second time. The mixture will become still thicker; and the third time, place the vessel upon the fire, and let the mixture come to a boil. The bran of the malt is now to be separated by passing the fluid through a fine sieve. The soup is now ready for use.

Concentrated milk is a most excellent article of diet for the infant, and the author is happy to say that he has found marked beneficial results from its use in many instances.

Carrot pap is recommended by Dr. Grumprecht, of Hamburg, and is prepared by mixing one ounce of finely-grated, full-grown carrots with two cupfuls of water, and let stand for twelve hours, frequently stirring in the meantime.

It is now to be strained, and the residue compressed, that the juice may also be obtained. To the fluid thus obtained is to be added finely-powdered biscuit, crackers, or farina, that a pap may be made, and then placed on a slow fire, and heated *short* of the *boiling point*, that the albumen may *not* be coagulated. Sweeten with pure white sugar, and it is ready for use. It is advised not to use the carrot pap if there is any tendency to diarrhœa.

Another method of preparing the pap is, to take one ounce of grated yellow carrot, and two drachms of powdered biscuit, with two cupfuls of soft water. Mix and let stand in a cool place for twelve hours; then strain, add a little salt, and sweeten with sugar-candy. Warm the pap, and let the infant take its meal from the nursing-bottle.

The author has found the following preparation to agree well with the infant, and also useful as a curative in diarrhœa:

Take a teacupful of dry flour, and tie it up closely in a cloth or rag, and then boil constantly for two consecutive hours, at the end of this time, the flour will have been formed into a ball (the centre of which will be hard and dry), which is to be grated into a powder, sweetened, and mixed with milk to the consistency of gruel when it is ready for use.

Water that is cool, not absolutely cold, is as necessary, as much desired, and as agreeable to the infant as to those who are more matured, especially during the teething processes when the gums are irritated, and the mouth hot and feverish.

Wet nurses are sometimes obtained to supply the mother's place to the unfortunate infant, but it is almost impossible to to find one, just at the time she is wanted, who will suitably fill all the necessary conditions, as these are numerous; and the attempt to comply with them all, opens up so many avenues to deception, that, even those who are most skilled in the selection of such a nurse are easily imposed upon. But, if it is determined to employ a *wet nurse*, let it be remembered that the milk changes, as we have already seen, in both its qualities and properties with the increasing age of the infant, therefore, it is one of the essential conditions that the nurse should be the mother of an infant that is of the same age as the one deprived of its own mother's breast. If this condition is not complied with, evil, rather than beneficial results, will ensue. A newly-born infant, if nursed by a mother whose babe is several months old, is likely to become scrofulous. The nurse, and the mother whose place she is to supply, should be of the same build and temperament; as the babe of a short, heavy-set woman, will not thrive at the breast of a tall, spare woman; and the reverse of this is also true. It is quite easy to be deceived in regard to the quantity and quality of the milk. If the infant of the nurse is in a thriving condition, it is evidence that the milk is of sufficient quantity, and of a quality that agrees with her own babe; but when she takes another infant to her breast, it does not necessarily follow that these conditions of the milk will continue to be adequate to the necessities of both infants; on the contrary, the milk may become deteriorated in quality, while it increases in quantity, and neither of the infants will thrive so well as the nurse's own did, before taking the second one to her breast. Under these circumstances, the nurse will naturally, in a gradual and an unconscious manner, be led to favor her own babe. The one will seem to thrive, while the effect of this slow process of starvation on the other, will be attributed to other causes, for the nurse, honestly thinking, but egregiously mistaken, declares her impartial treatment of the two infants. These effects will gather upon the little sufferer, and hurry it off to its final resting-place before the parents are aware of the perils which surround their offspring. It is scarcely necessary to observe that the nurse should be a healthy woman. And this is not, at all times, an easy matter to determine, as disease, either hereditary or acquired, may exist in the blood in a latent form, or the history of the nurse may be so imperfect, or lacking altogether, as to deceive those who are most expert in such examinations. Therefore, the only method of securing the infant from becoming infected, is *not* to employ a *wet-nurse.* The bosom should be full, round, and plump, with not the least sore about the nipple.

It is of the utmost importance that the nurse should be kind, gentle, quiet, willing, and subservient in the discharge of all her duties, honest and faithful in all of her trusts. It is only by a certainty that the nurse possesses these qualities that the infant is saved from the effects of many hurtful and deceptive irregularities of the nursery. She should be free from the habit of flying into fits of passion and outbursts of temper, as these conditions of the mind exercise very deleterious effects upon the blood, and, consequently, the nourishing fluid. The following instance constitutes a marked illustration of the effects of passion upon the milk and the consequent results to the offspring, mentioned by the physican to the king of Saxony, in his work previously referred to:

"A carpenter fell into a quarrel with a soldier, billeted in his house, and was set upon by the latter with his drawn sword. The wife of the carpenter at first trembled with fear and terror, and then threw herself furiously between the combatants, wrested the sword from the soldier's hand, broke it in pieces, and threw it away. During the tumult some neighbors came in and separated the men. While in this state of strong excitement, the mother took up her child from the cradle, where it lay playing, and in the most perfect health, never having had a moment's illness, she gave it the breast, and in so doing sealed its fate. In a few minutes the infant left off sucking, became restless, panted, and *sank dead on its mother's bosom.* The physician, who was instantly called in, found the infant lying in the cradle as if asleep, and with its features undisturbed; but all his resources were fruitless. It was irrecoverably gone."*

This, although an extreme case, should be a warning to those mothers and nurses who indulge in outbursts of passion, for such conduct will surely bring evil to the offspring.

OF THE AIR THE INFANT BREATHES.

The absolute necessity of the infant breathing a pure atmosphere has been duly considered, and clearly shown by the success which attended the adoption of Dr. Clarke's suggestion *to ventilate the wards and admit* PURE AIR THROUGHOUT THE BUILDING *of the Dublin Lying-in Hospital.*

OF THE CLOTHING.

In clothing the body, we have two objects in view: *first*, to conceal nakedness; *second*, to maintain that degree of temperature which is normal to a healthy state of the economy. In attaining the first of these, care is to be taken that the garments are so constructed and adjusted to the body as not to prevent the free movements of the extremities, the movements of the chest-walls in breathing, or to interfere with the circulation of the blood. The *second* object is to be considered in determining the kind of material of which the garments are to be made, and the amount of clothing with which

---

*See COMBE on Infancy.

the infant is to be clad. The necessity of duly regarding the temperature of the young is rendered more manifest, when we consider : *first*, that the normal temperature of the infant is somewhat higher than that of the adult. It is this fact that causes the nurse to exclaim : "Why, how hot the baby is! A baby is as hot as an oven." *Second*, the smallness of the quantity of blood, and the thinness of the tissues which intervene between the blood and the atmosphere afford less protection against chilling influences. From these circumstances, the infant will, when exposed to a low temperature, become chilled much sooner than the adult. As is the case with water, a drop exposed to a low temperature will freeze immediately, whereas a large body will require a much lower temperature, and a longer period of time to accomplish its consolidation. Many infants are annually lost for the want of a strict attention to these facts, and although fashion and custom are blindly followed, and, *with procrustean cruelty*, rigidly adhered to, instead of being adapted to the wants of the infant, mothers wonder why their children do not thrive! "Certainly, says Dr. Meigs, I have reason to think that thousands of lives are annually sacrificed to mere fashion in dress, whether of those that are born in hot, or those that come into the world in the cold seasons." This immense sacrifice of human life can easily be arrested by supplying the necessities of the infant, instead of using it as a toy to display a foolish, extravagant expenditure of money, in order to gratify a morbid taste in dress.

It is impossible to indicate the quantity of clothing the infant should wear, because the several latitudes vary so widely in degrees of temperature, as well as in the seasons of the year, and of the extent of comfort supplied by the house in which the infant may dwell. These circumstances, when duly considered in connection with the degree of temperature normal to infantile life, will be the best guides as to the amount of clothing the infant should wear. The organization of the adult, as we have already seen, is not so easily impressed by the changes of temperature as that of the infant; hence, the nurse cannot determine, by her own feelings, as to the warmth of the infant, but must examine by touch, and observe every manifestation of cold, and clothe the infant according to its necessities. The head should be left bare, except when taken out of doors; then a hood, cap, or bonnet, should be used to protect the head from the sun, wind, or cold; and these will determine the character of the head-covering. Experience has taught us it is best for the infant to wear a flannel or woolen skirt through the first two years, as the changes of temperature in the infant take place too suddenly when it is exposed to a higher or lower degree of temperature. When the infant has arrived at the hot days of its third summer, the flannel may be replaced by lighter garments, as the continuance of the flannel skirt would become oppressive.

OF WEANING.

Many evils of dentition may be averted by strict attention to the time and manner of weaning the infant. When the incisors are through, which, as we have seen at page 86, is during the tenth month, the infant should be allowed food, in very small quantities and at long intervals, other than mother's milk. Such feeding is not only harmless, but is actually demanded by the workings of nature in the infant. Early feedings may consist of bread boiled in milk, with a pinch of salt added, a roasted potato mixed with gravy, chicken broth, soft-boiled eggs, rice pudding, arrow-root boiled in water with an addition of milk. Such feeding may be continued until the appearance of the anterior molars, which takes place from the twelfth to the fourteenth month, when a stronger diet may be introduced by way of meats and vegetables. If these are found to agree with the infant, its hunger will be appeased with a dietary that is more agreeable to its taste and compatible with its organism, and the withdrawal of the breast becomes an easy matter. It must be observed that this is to be done in the fall, winter, or early spring, and *never during the hot months*.

The infant who is blessed, by having all these conditions fully and properly filled, will pass through the teething process with but little trouble, whereas, the one who has not been so fortunately circumstanced, will suffer more or less severely, if not removed by death.

PART V.

THE INFANT IN SICKNESS.

However healthy and free from hereditary taints the parents may be, and healthy and vigorous the infant may come into the world, and actively its organs may perform their functions, the healthy infant is liable to be overtaken by *sickness or disease*. And when this unfortunate circumstance occurs, it then becomes necessary to provide means for the comfort and restoration of the infant to a state of health. To supply it with those things which are essential to its *comfort*, is the duty of the mother, or nurse, and constitutes *nursing;* whereas the means of restoration consists in the medication or treatment of the case, and this is the duty of the medical attendant.

When the infant is discovered to be ailing, the first duty of the nurse is to provide a chamber suitable for a "*sick-room.*" There are several circumstances which add materially to the fitness of the chamber for the habitation of the sick. Its location on the second or third floor will secure a purer atmosphere, and a better circulation of air throughout the room, than if situated on the first floor of the building. The air should be admitted in such a manner that it will *not* fall upon the patient, when the bed is placed near a window, and the sash lowered from above. Neither should the patient be placed in a draft, as between two open windows.

A circumstance that is in the highest degree essential to the welfare of the infant in sickness, is quietude, that the nervous system may be tranquil and the sleep refreshing. These will render the medicines prompt and efficient in their action upon the system, and, therefore, a chamber should be selected in which the stillness is undisturbed by noise from any cause whatever, such as a busy street. In conducting the household affairs, the ringing of the door-bell, the tread of footsteps in the hall, and the constant inquiries in regard to the condition of the patient, should be avoided.

The maintenance in cold weather of a uniform temperature throughout the room, is a matter of the utmost importance, and the author has met with more than one instance in which he was forced to ascribe the cause of the illness and death of his patient to *a lack of uniformity in the temperature of the apartment* which the infant occupied. The lack of a uniformity in the temperature of the chamber may be due either to the very high ceiling, badly-fitting doors or window-sash, the construction of the chimney, or the setting of the grate. A chamber so imperfectly warmed will be uncomfortable as we go towards, or farther from, the fire; "one side will burn, and the other freeze." Such rooms are *wholly unfit to be inhabited by either the young or older persons, even when in health.* If the grate is faulty, let a stove be introduced into the chamber, and an open vessel filled with water kept constantly on the stove, that a due amount of vapor may be maintained in the atmosphere. The temperature of the room should range from 60° to 70° Fahr., according to the condition of the patient.

After the selection of a room in the residence that is most susceptible of being made to comply with the above conditions, it should be thoroughly cleansed, made inviting and cheerful by brightening the ceiling, and the distribution of a few pictures about the walls, and supplied with those articles of furniture that are necessary only to the welfare of the patient and the convenience of the attendants. These should consist of a bed, a table, a few chairs, and a washstand with drawers; book-case and books, sofa and lounge, are only to be *tolerated* in the sick room. The bed should consist of a child's crib, with rockers, furnished with a mattress—never with a feather-bed—a pillow, sheets and blankets. The portable furniture should consist of a ewer, constantly filled with soft water, a basin, a slop-bowl, a supply of towels, clean rags, soap, and a bathing sponge. On the table there should be a pitcher of water for the administering of medicine, several tumblers—*not goblets*—table, dessert, and teaspoons, a bowl of sugar, writing paper, pen and ink—and the medicines to be used should also find place on the table. If the family should be in the country, or remote from a drug-store, there should be conveniently at hand a camphor bottle, filled, with the gum dissolved in *alcohol* instead of whiskey, a vial of laudanum, paregoric, castor oil, sweet oil, syrup of ipecac, a box of mustard, and a small quantity of good whiskey.

After the chamber has been thus selected, prepared-

and furnished, let the infant be undressed and reclothed with a clean, dry napkin, a flannel gown, extending six inches below the feet, with sleeves, and a single button at the throat, and a like garment made of muslin will complete the dressing. The infant is now ready for the physician. Instead of this systematic course of preparation, it occasionally occurs that the family, in a sudden manner, concludes that "it is best that the doctor should see the baby," and precipitately sends a messenger "for the doctor," who, upon his arrival, finds the family and servants busily engaged in making hurried preparations for his reception, and the infant bundled, buttoned, and pinned up in half a dozen skirts, in a manner to make it almost impossible to get at the chest or the abdomen with a view of making an exploration of the parts, and, in place of hearing a quiet and concise history of the case, he must, with the patience of Job, listen to many apologies for the house being so much out of order, and for the baby being so untidy. And if the physician should chance to be a man of little experience in practice, and in meeting with such precipitate calls, he will become so confused as to know neither how or where to commence his investigations.

The foregoing preparations for the sick may be considered as altogether superfluous, and the infant is suffered to pass from health into the midst of a fever of several weeks duration, whereas, if the family should be expecting an entertainment of only a few hours, there will be several days spent in making preparations. But the infant must pass through its sufferings without the slightest preparation whatever having been made for its illness, and, perhaps, for the lack of which, it may perish. Very much, indeed, will depend upon the orderly manner in which we enter upon the management and treatment of a case of sickness, that everything may move along smoothly and well-timed, otherwise everything will be done roughly out of time and place. There will be many things in the room occupying space that ought to be given to pure and wholesome atmosphere for the benefit of the patient, and many kindly visiting neighbors polluting the air with the effluvia from their lungs and bodies, and, still worse, with their many ignorant and incongruous suggestions as to the management and treatment of the case, by which the nurse is diverted from her immediate duties, and is led to disregard her instructions, and the physician is so annoyed that it is impossible for him to follow up his train of reflections in the analysis of the history and symptoms of the case, that he may arrive at a correct diagnosis; and rather he will be caused to omit the due consideration of one or more symptoms, as the conditions of the fontanel,* the pupils, the rythm of the respiratory movements, the pulse, the temperature, the mode of attack, and many other circumstances that are of equal importance. Or, in case the infant should be seized with a spasm, and an assistant is directed to obtain the mustard, a plate and a knife, for the preparation of a plaster to be applied for the relief of the sufferer, she will go stumbling over chairs or other articles that crowd the room, or be hindered by visiting friends who have just come in to see the baby, and she goes down stairs to the pantry, and finally, when she returns, it is discovered that another trip is necessary, as the assistant had forgotten one of the articles, or, in her haste, had brought the salt cellar instead of the mustard.

---

*The space between the bones of the cranium.

When the physician arrives, he should be met by the mother, who will give him a full history of the case—*i. e.*, *who* is sick, the age of the patient, when it was taken sick, the mode of attack, the condition of its health previous to its sickening, and its condition since; and what, if anything, in the way of domestic practice or by the advice of a physician, had been done for the sufferer. In imparting this information to the physician, the mother should never exaggerate in any particular, as, "He was so hot, I thought he would surely burn up;" but state precisely what she had discovered to be the case. Neither should she give the physician *her diagnosis of the case*, for two reasons: *First*, she, without a medical education, is not competent to make a diagnosis; *second*, it is necessary for the physician to arrive at his diagnosis through a process of induction, that he may not only know what the disease is, but also its nature and extent; and he must arrive at a knowledge of these conditions through an analysis of the history, the symptoms, and indications of all the circumstances which surround his patient. After the interview with the mother, he is to be conducted to the sick chamber, where he should find his patient in the crib, and a fortunate circumstance, indeed, if asleep. *There should be none other in the chamber but the mother or nurse.* The approach of the physician should be easy and gentle, that the infant may lie undisturbed while the physician carefully notes the position of his patient; the condition of the *fontanel* if natural or otherwise; the features, if expressive of pain; the skin, if moistened with perspiration—if so, is it general, or confined to the forehead; the lips, if pale, or red, or dry; the eyes, if closed or partly open; the hands, if closed, and the thumb embraced within the fingers; the respiratory movements, regular or irregular, prolonged and deep, or short, shallow, and rapid in succession, thoracic or abdominal; the passage of the air into the lungs, if attended with any unnatural sounds; the abdomen, if distended or flaccid; the pulse must be counted, and the character of the pulsation well noted, and now the temperature may be taken with the thermometer. The physician may now resort to the *third* source of knowledge of the condition of his patient, viz.: a physical examination of the body. For this purpose, he will have the mother to take the infant on a pillow in her lap, and proceed to percuss and auscultate the chest, with the view of ascertaining the condition of the lungs, the bronchial tubes, the pleura, and of the heart and its action; he will, with his hand, explore the abdomen for the detection of hardness, enlargement of any of the viscera, or the existence or non-existence of pain. Now, let it be borne in mind, that these symptoms may belong to several different diseases; for instance, fever is associated with inflammation of the brain, lungs, bronchial tubes, and bowels; and the physician is to arrive at his diagnosis through a process of reasoning from the data he has obtained from the methods of inquiry just described, and is then to establish a course of treatment most consistent with the nature of the case. It will be observed that our patient has been examined, the diagnosis made, and the treatment determined upon without a single word being spoken in the room. All the necessary conversation transpired before the physician entered the chamber. Now contrast the foregoing scene with the following:

"John, go to Mrs. A.'s and tell her the baby is sick, and to come over; and then go to Mrs. B.'s; tell them to come very soon, for I am expecting the doctor every minute."

Those ladies make due haste, that they may anticipate the arrival of the physician with their inquiries concerning the disease, and the remedies already given, with their suggestions to be made to the doctor, who now arrives to find the chamber in the condition as already described, with the neighbors present—the mother trotting the bundled-up baby on her knee, to quiet its excitement from the presence and noise of so many strangers. Under these circumstances, the physician can do no more than feel the pulse, the forehead, and possibly the abdomen; and no sooner does he commence this *very imperfect examination*, than one of the ladies will say:

"Doctor, has it much fever?"

"No, madam, not much."

Another:

"Doctor, is the pulse very high?"

"Tolerably so, madam."

"Well, doctor, don't you think the baby has pneumonia?"

"Well, madam, I cannot say, just now, that I do."

"Well, I thought from its breathing that it had; and as our baby has had pneumonia, I was going to tell you what I did for mine."

And the mother will become more interested in the conversation between the neighbors and the doctor, than she is in his making a careful examination of the child; and, for a very good reason, she thinks her friends are *spurring* the doctor up to his *duty*, and making *valuable* suggestions that otherwise would escape his attention. This may be considered as an overdrawn picture, but the author can assure the reader that it is as true to instances of almost daily occurrence, as a photograph taken by the most expert artist can be of the best subject that he ever had to sit before his instrument. And thus humanity is daily trifled with—*even to the destruction of life itself.* The author would respectfully say to the mother of the sick infant: Let your neighbors stay at home; and to the neighbors; Keep away from the sick infant, and pursue the following course:

August 20th, 1879.

My Dear Mrs. B———: I was much pained to learn this morning that your baby is so sick as to require the attention of your physician, and sincerely hope it will soon recover; but, in the meantime, my services and anything that I have which will contribute to the comfort of your darling infant is at your disposal.

Your sympathizing friend,
Grace Thomas.

No direct answer to this note is required. Circumstances may, however, cause the following to be necessary:

August 23d, 1879.

Mrs. Thomas—*Dear Madam:* I am sorry to say that the baby is no better; and we are very much exhausted from fatigue and loss of sleep. I hope it will not be asking too much for your assistance through the night.

Your friend,
B———.

Mrs. B———: I will be at your service at 8 P. M.
Grace Thomas.

Let all the visitors to the house of the sick be received in any room other than that occupied by the patient—*if it is the kitchen. Company* have no business in the sick-room; it is *a nuisance, a hindrance, and a torment to the patient.*

THE INFANT IN SICKNESS. 119

The physician having now made his diagnosis, and determined upon the plan of treatment, it becomes the duty of the nurse to carry out the directions precisely as ordered. That this end may be attained, the physician must give the instructions in a manner that is clear, concise, comprehensive, complete in all of the details, and with such a degree of precision as will leave nothing to the option of the nurse, thus: You will place the blister immediately over the left nipple; after the lapse of one hour and a half, you will examine it every *twenty* minutes until you discover little watery pimples, then remove the plaster, and with a little warm soap-suds and a soft sponge wash all the ointment that may remain, completely off, and dress the blister with a muslin cloth and sweet oil. Give one of the powders every three hours, until the bowels shall have moved the fourth time; and a teaspoonful of the contents of the vial every time the clock strikes, unless the infant is asleep. You will continue this until my return, to-morrow morning at 9 o'clock.

The nurse should now be attentive to the administering of the medicines, and all other conditions essential to the well-being of the patient, and note well each phase of the case and things that may occur. When the physician returns, he should be met and receive a full account of all that transpired during his absence, after which he must be conducted to the chamber, be seated, and make the same observations as before; and let it be again observed, that it is a matter of no small moment that he should be let alone in his observations and examinations, therefore, let silence prevail. Do not disturb him by asking questions, or conversing in the room. Such indiscretions have been the cause of the death of many infants. The physician will again give his directions to the nurse, and let all the foregoing precautions be rigidly observed throughout the entire course of treatment. By these means, the termination will, most likely, be in a happy restoration; but, if an overruling providence, for some good purpose, should take the infant to the land of departed spirits, both the parents and physician will feel satisfied that they have coöperated in directing their efforts in a manner most favorable to bring about a cure. Hence, they will not have to reflect upon themselves for not having fully discharged their duty.

Medicines are administered to infants either in powder, syrup, elixir, or solution in water. If the powder is small in quantity, the tip of the finger may be moistened and then pressed upon the powder, which is thus transferred to the child's tongue, and then give the patient a little water or the breast. Fluids are given by drops, or a teaspoonful is more convenient, as it saves the trouble of counting the number of drops to be given at each dosing. Medicines are usually directed to be administered at regular intervals, and the nurse should closely observe the time, that the medicine may be given precisely at the appointed hour. Medicines are also administered by injections under the skin and in the bowel.

Having considered the circumstances demanded by our infant when sick, and the way in which it should be managed through the period of its illness, we will now return to its personal consideration.

Infantile life is susceptible of being divided into two periods. The first is from birth to the end of the first year, or at the usual time of weaning; and the second is from weaning until the eruption of the temporary teeth, which is complete at the end of the second year. The two periods may be designated as the *first* and *second* year of infancy. It is not time alone that marks these periods, but also the stages of development peculiar to the first and second year of human existence. In the first the tissues are thinner and softer, and the vital functions are performed in a more feeble manner than in the second year. For these reasons the infant in his first months will more readily succumb under disease, and when laboring under high inflammatory action will not endure depleting treatment so well as when farther advanced in life. This enfeebled power of resistance and of endurance is compensated for by an exemption from disease found in the freedom of the organism from an accumulation of effete matter, which clogs the wheels of the machine. It is, as we have already seen, the existence or the retention of accumulated effete matter in the system that is the cause of many diseases, especially those which are characterized by an eruption of the skin, as in measles and scarlet fever. The freedom of the infant, in its first months, from such matter remaining in the blood and tissues is due to two circumstances: *first*, the simplicity of its food as compared with the complexity and variety of that which is given to the infant when taken from the breast; *second*, the older one can exercise itself freely by walking, running and playing, which causes a greater wear of the muscles and other tissues of the body, and hence a greater amount of effete matter must pass through the blood, whereas the exercise of the younger infant is confined to the movement of its carriage, to being carried in its nurse's arms, and to the movements of its extremities while lying upon its back; therefore there is far less effete matter to pass through its blood to be eliminated.

Attention has already been called to the importance of thoroughly cleansing the eyes of the newly-born, and that this should be accomplished without the use of soap, lest it should get into the eyes, and result in inflammation. This inflammation, should it occur, may be relieved by bathing with warm water or milk fresh from the breast. If, however, relief should not be immediately obtained, the mother should not delay in procuring medical advice, for by neglect the lids will swell, close, and will keep the eyeballs hot, the inflammation will spread with great rapidity, pus will be formed in large quantities, and destruction of the tissues ensue by ulceration, and a loss of vision as the dire result.

Daily attention should be given to the infant's mouth, as the sucking process, combined with the presence of an accumulation of acrid matter in the mouth, will cause the thin and delicate tissues to inflame and ulcerate, and this will excite a like condition of the nipple. As a precautionary measure against such evils let the mother constantly have at hand a vial of *liquor calcis saccharatus*. She will put one teaspoonful of the liquor into a tumbler (*goblets should never be used in the sick room*) filled with SOFT water,* and, with a soft mop, cleanse the mouth of the infant, as well as her nipples, morning and evening.

The natural passage for the air to the lungs is through the nostrils, and, we have seen in Part III, the infant is not sufficiently developed to be conscious of its necessities and must, therefore, depend upon its instinctive desires and reflex action of the nervous system for the maintenance of the vital forces in their operative functions. Strict attention

---

*The mixture must be freshly prepared upon each occasion.

must be paid to this passage that it may not become obstructed, either by the accumulation of mucus or swelling of the mucous membrane from a "*bad cold*," or *coryza*. If such an obstruction should occur, the infant will not open its mouth that the air may find a passage to the lungs, nor is it practical to force the mouth open, as the infant will draw the tongue backward in such manner as to close the larynx. Mucus may be removed with the head of a pin and its accumulation prevented by keeping the nostril well oiled by the introduction of lard into the passages; the heat of the part will cause the lard to become sufficiently thin to flow through the passage. When a stoppage of the passage occurs from inflammatory swelling of the membranes, a most excellent remedy is to mix five parts of sub-carbonate of bismuth with one part of powdered gum arabic and let it be used as a snuff, or put it in a quill or a small glass tube, or a straw, and introduce it into the nostril and blow the powder over the diseased parts. The author has never found this remedy fail in producing a cure, even in the severest cases. The following is so forcibly illustrative of the importance of keeping the nares open that the author feels he would be remiss in the discharge of his duty to the reader not to give it a place here:

"A few years since I[*] attended a lady in North Tenth street, in this city, who gave birth to a healthy, though small and delicate, child. It did well for some days, and then became affected with the slight coryza so common among infants, on account of which it was kept warm, and the monthly nurse applied the usual remedy of greasing the nostrils at bed time. The mucous secretion of the coryza gradually collected about the apertures and formed lampers, or

---

[*] Dr. C. D. Meigs, of Philadelphia.

plugs, which filled up the entire nostrils as completely as if they had been filled up with a vial cork. The parents found the child apparently dying, and members of the family, from different parts of the city, were assembled to witness the decease of their young relative.

"Being notified by an urgent message of the dangerous condition of the infant, I hastened to the house, and, finding the friends solemnized by the approaching event, I also was at first convinced that the child was about to perish.

"It breathed after very long intervals, during which there was no apparent attempt to respire, and I noticed, that when it did make its aspirations, they were very sudden, rapid, and violent, after which it relapsed into its non-respiring condition.

"I did not understand the nature of the case, but I remarked that it could not be spasmatic nor pseudo-morphous laryngitis, nor, indeed, any laryngeal affection, because, when it did respire, it did so with full freedom and perfection, which could not be predicated of any affection of the larynx, of the bronchi, or the lungs,

"In the doubt in which I was placed, I took the child on its pillow upon my knee, in order to inspect it more closely, an inspection which left me no room to doubt that the obstruction was in the nares, and upon a closer examination, I found that the nares were entirely stopped up, as I before remarked. By means of the head of a pin, I removed the plug from the external nostril, but I could not free the deeper parts of the passages.

"Seeing that the child was about to die (and I have at this moment no doubt that it was, but for the rescue, within half an hour of its death), I lifted it in my hands, and, applying my mouth to the nostrils, and blowing violently into the openings, I loosened, and discharged the plugs into its pharynx, after which it was in a few minutes perfectly well, and I had no further trouble with it.

"I saw," says this doctor, "a little child perish in North Sixth street, a few years ago, from this cause. He had great aspirations at long intervals; the nostrils were entirely closed, not by mucus, but by sub-mucus infiltration, bringing the sides into contact, and closing the passage. As long as I could sit before him, preventing his tongue from touching his soft palate, and keeping his lips from closing, so as to admit air into his larynx, the child was perfectly well; but, as it was impossible, on account of his resistance and struggles, to sit before him with a spoon on his tongue for many consecutive hours, it was necessary to abandon him to his fate, and he perished a few hours after I left him, persisting to breath through an impractical passage in his nostrils.

"I saw a fine child, nearly two years old, perish, in January, 1845, from nearly a similar cause.

"Perhaps the reader," continues Dr. Meigs, "perhaps some spectator, might doubt the propriety of the explanation of the cause of the death in these cases. I recommend such cavillers to repeat the attempt of persisting to breathe through the nostrils closed by the finger and thumb, after which all doubts must vanish from the mind."

During the first year, it is designed for the infant to obtain its nourishment from its mother's breast, and that by sucking, for which purpose we find that the mouth of the child is peculiarly adapted, by its shallowness, shortness of the jaws, delicacy of the muscles, and the absence of teeth. These conditions enable the infant to bring its mouth into a position best adapted to drawing or sucking in its food. But as it advances in life, the operations of nature prepare it for the circumstances and conditions which are then to surround it. Therefore, we observe the lower jaw grow longer, and from a horizontal to an oblique downward direction, which gives length to the chin and space for the thickening gums and coming teeth. The face grows broader, and the cavity of the mouth larger for the reception and mastication of the food. The muscles become stronger and thicker, that the teeth may be applied with sufficient force to crush and masticate the food, preparatory for the digestive processes. The most obvious and interesting change which takes place in the mouth is the appearance of the teeth. As we have already considered the history of teeth development, and the best way of managing the infant to prepare it for a safe passage through the process, it now remains to consider *teething* in relation to the general health, and its management during *dentition*.

Notwithstanding the eruption of the teeth is a physiological process, yet it is occasionally attended with such disturbances as to receive the appellation of *difficult dentition*, which sometimes results in death. Such cases are attended with slight febrile movements, which manifest themselves in an accelerated pulse and redness of the cheeks and gums, and the irritable character of the fever is shown by the increased flow of saliva, more frequent intestinal discharges of a thin consistency, containing mucus and bile, attended with nausea and vomiting. When these symptoms begin to present themselves, the advice of the family physician should be obtained without delay. The flow of saliva and the increased discharges of the bowels are means by which nature endeavors to relieve herself of the disturbed state of the system, and if astringent medicines are administered, with a view of arresting the discharges, very grave results will ensue. Also, the healing up of those sores which are frequently found behind the ears of teething infants. These should be let alone, for by these means the infant is saved from that degree of irritation which would result in convulsions, paralysis and inflammation of the brain, and death.

There are two remedies that can be applied locally, which, in many cases, give such marked relief as to act like magic: *First*, is to rub the gum with a crystal of bromide potassium, which is a very simple method, and can be resorted to by the mother; the second is to lance, or incise freely, the gum. It is not an uncommon occurrence to meet with mothers whose sympathies become so much aroused as to protest against the performance of this simple operation; but if they had a correct appreciation of the beneficial results which accrue to the infant from so efficient, though so simple an operation, their sympathies would move them to have the operation performed, when necessary, without delay. The author will not detain the reader with a recital of some of the many instances of marked, and even surprising, results that followed the free use of the knife, in his own experience; but will cite the following case from Dr. Condie, who says:

"A curious case is related by Robert, in his treatise on the Principal Objects of Medicine, illustrative as well of one of the effects of difficult dentition, as of the division of the gums. We give it upon the authority of Carault, not having seen the work of Robert: 'A child, after having suffered greatly from difficult dentition, apparently died, and was laid out for interment. Lemonnier, having some business at the house of the nurse with whom the child resided, after fulfilling the object of his visit, was desirous of ascertaining the condition of the alveola. He accordingly made a free incision through the gums. On preparing to pursue further his examination, he perceived the child to open its eyes, and give other indications of life. He immediately called for assistance. The shroud was removed from the body, and by careful and persevering attention, the child's life was saved. The teeth in due time made their appearance, and its health was fully restored.'"

From the writer's own experience in the results obtained from this *simple* and *harmless* operation, as well as from a knowledge of the effects upon the nervous system of the pressure of the teeth against the gum, he has no doubt that the above reported rescue from a pending death is literally true. The author would cite the case of a near relative, who lay at the point of death for six weeks, attended by several physicians, and was considered as hopeless. Finally, it was decided to *freely incise the gums.* Within an hour's time the patient was in her usual health, engaged with her toys, and required no further treatment.

We have seen from time to time the importance of the infant being constantly supplied with a pure and wholesome atmosphere; and when, in dentition (which continues through the whole of the second year), we consider that the heart is still active in the performance of its function the free circulation of the blood; of the ascendancy of the nervous system over the organism, and the rapidity with which the developing processes are going on, under the exciting influences of almost every object, and stranger, with which the infant may come in contact; and the mind, which is now so far developed as to endeavor to comprehend the use of objects and the meaning of sounds—under this excitement the *will* begins to determine the movements of the body, when it is amusing and interesting to see the little creature with its tottering steps, arms extended, eyes and mouth agape, and quivering head, making strenuous efforts to arrive at an object but a few inches distant. Cannot we see in this state of the infant the utmost importance of an atmosphere free from all impurities, that the blood and tissues may be duly oxidized? Let us for a moment witness the effects of transferring the healthy infant into a room that is badly ventilated, and perhaps a smoky chimney, with several grown persons still further poisoning the air with the effluvia from their bodies, and suffocating the infant by crowding around it—and that, too, more for their own curiosity than for any good they may do for the infant. Under these circumstances, we will witness a scene quite different from the one just described, and in which the infant loses its energies, becomes pale, languid, and lifeless. As pure air and free ventilation are so essential to the healthy infant, how much more so must it be when the vital forces are weakened by disease. Therefore, too much care cannot be observed in securing to the teething infant a volume of pure air, freely and constantly circulating about the person.

The illness of the infant will be recognized by the *semiology* or signs of disease. Some diseases are ushered in, in such manner as to leave no doubt that the infant is sick. It may be seized with a convulsion, a chill and fever, or with a fever accompanied by great prostration. Again, disease may be so insidious in its approach as to escape attention until it explodes in such violence as will imperil the life of the infant. A remarkable case of this kind came under the observation of the author in the case of a most interesting child of three years of age. The writer was at the time living in the country. He was, on a Saturday afternoon, a mile distant from his home when he found a gentleman friend sitting in his yard, under a shade tree, with the child playing upon the green—the only young child in a family of grown sons and daughters, consequently a pet. Here the author stopped to enjoy a social chat, when the child came playing around, seeking to be noticed by him, who seated the child upon his lap and, by accident, placed one hand upon the back and the other upon the chest. There was a slight abnormity in the rythm of the chest movements, which caused the ear to be placed to the chest, whereupon the lungs were detected to be in the first stage of inflammation, or pneumonia. As the father had asked to be excused until he could finish a short paragraph in a paper which he had in his hand, this short examination escaped his attention. Just at the conclusion of the reading another mutual friend entered and engaged us both in an interesting conversation of an hour's duration, which caused the condition of the child to escape the memory of the observer, who went to his home without mentioning the danger of the child to the father. On the next morning, Sunday, at 10 o'clock, a messenger came in great haste to summon the author to see the child, whom he reported to be in a dying condition. It is needless to say that the author felt conscience-stricken for neglecting to inform the father of the condition of a child upon whom was centered so much affection by a large and devoted family. Upon arriving at the bedside of the patient he was found to be prostrate, speechless, pale, with purple spots here and there, threatened with convulsions and immediate death. In these trying hours consolation was found in the application of remedies which caused the threatening dangers gradually to pass away, with a restoration of the child to a state of perfect health. From this we may learn the importance of not treating too lightly slight indications of disease which often appear in the young.

COLIC.

This is, of all other complaints, the one with which the infant is most frequently afflicted, and occasions the mother many anxious hours and wakeful nights. COLIC implies violent pains in the abdomen, the word being derived from the Greek, *Kolikos*, from *Kolon*, the colon or large intestine; it, therefore, conveys no definite idea of the cause of the suffering. And as pains are excited in the bowels of the infant by a number of causes which vary widely from each other, and the means of obtaining relief are equally varied; it is, therefore, an unfortunate circumstance, that all pains which occur in the abdomen are grouped under the one name, COLIC. The infant is thus subjected to repeated dosings of medicines and nostrums, and the vague question, "*what is good for the colic?*" is often asked the physician, who prescribing without seeing the patient and learning the cause of the pain, his remedy fails in producing relief, and discredit is thereby brought upon himself and the profession.

Of the several varieties of colic to which the infant is subject, we may mention:

A.—Neuralgia, or nervous colic.
B.—Spasmodic colic.
C.—Bilious colic.
D.—Flatulent, or windy colic.
E.—Inflammatory colic.

A.—*Neuralgia*, or *nervous* colic, is recognized by the regularity of its attack, which occurs most generally in the afternoon, and, in many instances, at precisely the same hour of the day. This form of colic is not necessarily accompanied with derangements of the digestive organs, and the bowels may naturally and regularly perform their daily functions.

As this is characterized by a periodicity, quinine may be administered in small doses three times a day with advantage. The moment the infant is seized with the pains, let the little sufferer be laid upon a blanket spread over the nurse's lap, with its hips well exposed to a hot fire, and administer a powder composed of the sixth of a grain of Dover's powder and one third of a grain of ipecac. In a surprisingly short time it will fall into a profound sleep, accompanied with a profuse perspiration. It is now to be laid in its cradle to sleep, freed from its suffering. This treatment is to be promptly repeated upon each occurence of the attack, and the fire, the blanket, and the powder must be at hand that no delay be made in giving the suffering infant immediate relief. By this course of treatment entire freedom from the attacks will be obtained. The author has known instances in which the daily attacks would occur for sixty consecutive days.

B.—*Spasmodic*, sometimes called *incidental*, colic. This form of the complaint is the result of temporary indigestion, of some unwholesome article of diet, of constipation, or of some cause that is not clearly definable.

This should be met with palliatives—opiates, hot baths, and mustard plasters to the abdomen. Fluid ext. of wild yam, administered in doses of three drops every two hours, is an effective remedy. After the patient has been relieved, as a precautionary measure, the bowels should be evacuated by a cathartic—calomel or podophylin. The latter should be given in doses of an eighth or sixth of a grain and repeated twice daily until the bowels are well purged.

C.—*Bilious Colic* results from an accumulation of bile and mucus in the stomach, accompanied with a coated tongue, and, frequently, fever.

A light emetic is the best means of relief. This should be accomplished with syrup of ipecac. The vomiting will, at once, relieve the suffering, and should be followed by a purgative, lest another attack should occur.

D.—*Flatulency, or wind colic* is the result of indigestion, and we have, in the preceding pages, endeavored to show the great importance of feeding the infant in accordance with the demands of nature. And the radical means of relieving the patient must be sought in correcting any irregularities in feeding the infant, or, in discovering the diet that is operating to his detriment.

Immediate relief is to be obtained through palliatives :—

$$\left. \begin{array}{l} \text{Simple Syrup} - - - \ ʒv \\ \text{Paregoric} - - - - - \ ʒi \\ \text{Sulphuric Ether} - - \ ʒii \end{array} \right\} \text{Mix.}$$

Dose.—From one-fourth to one teaspoonful, according to the age of the infant, to be repeated every three hours until relief is obtained. Such treatment must then be established as will give tone and strength to the organs.

E.—Inflammatory colic is accompanied with inflammation of the bowels. The inflammation may be the result of exposure, of a foreign substance within the intestine, of intersusception, *i. e.* the bowel folding in upon itself. The inflammation must be treated in an appropriate manner.

Finally, the colic may be due to the existence of two or more of the above causes, when the treatment will become more complicated, and may, with propriety, be termed a compound treatment, when much care must be exercised in the administration of medicine, that one remedy may not conflict with another, and thereby result in great harm.

FINIS.

INDEX.

	Page.
ABLUTION of the Newly-born,	68
ADVICE to Neighbors,	118
AGALAXY,	94
ALARM,	32–33
ALVINE DISCHARGES of the Fœtus,	47
ANCESTRY, Necessity of Learning the History of,	7
ANIMAL CONSTRUCTION of the Organization,	15
ASSOCIATIONS of the Pregnant Female,	40
ATIVISM,	31
AURICULAR SEPTUM,	66
AUTOPSY,	52
BAD COLDS,	123
BEE-STING, Case of,	34
BIRTH,	59
BLOOD, Female Pabulum of	Note—23
Male Pabulum of,	24
Circulation of,	66
Letting,	Note—44
BREASTS, Of the	73
Milk, Substitute for,	102
BREEDING BACK,	31
BROMIDE POTASSA,	126
CELL,	13
CARROT PAP,	102
CHEESE,	74
CITY CHILDREN,	9
CIRCUMSTANCES in which the Highest Order of Minds Most Frequently Appear,	18
CHILD-BEARING,	27–49
CIRCULATION of Air,	65

INDEX.

	Page.
Circulation of the Blood,	66
Chamber for the Sick,	110
Temperature of,	111
Clothing,	106
Cold, Effects of,	111
Colic, Varieties and Treatment,	131
Colostration,	71
Colostrum,	70–73
Confectionaries,	55
Concentrated Milk,	102
Coryza, or Catarrh	123
Country Children,	9
Cradle,	77
Crib,	77
Deformities, Congenital,	33
Degeneracy, Causes of,	Note—8
Dentition, Difficult,	126
Periods of,	86
Stages of,	86
Disease, Signs of,	129
Diseases, Hereditary,	15
Disposition,	16
Doctor's Directions, How Given,	119
Dress,	48
Fashion in,	51
For the Sick Infant,	113
Dynamic Condition of Matter,	31
Force,	31–33
Early Marrying,	27
Education, Effects of,	25
Eruption, Time of Teeth,	86
Eve,	5
Evils, Source of,	Note—8
In Improper Dressing,	49
Evil, Apprehension of,	32
Examination of the Sick Infant,	115

INDEX.

	Page.
EYES, Necessity of Cleansing,	122
FASHION,	51–107
FATIGUE,	55
FEAR, Effects of,	32
FEMALE Cultivation,	21
Education,	25
Duties,	21
FLOUR, Boiled,	103
FŒTUS in Utero,	28
FOOD, for the Pregnant Female,	42
FOOD, for the Infant,	72
FOOD, Improper,	98
GENIUS, Cause of Not Descending from Father to Son,	18
Men of,	17
GALACTAGOGUE,	95
GENERATIVE Organs,	73
GRECIAN-BEND, Walking,	52
GUMS, Cutting of,	126
GUM-TUBES,	101
HANDLING the Infant, Care in,	82
HEART,	66–81
HEARING, Sense of,	66
HEALTH, Laws of,	8
HEREDITARY DISEASES, Transmission of,	16
HEREDITARY TRAITS,	7
HIGHLY-GIFTED in the Opposite Sex is not a Factor in the Production of Superior Minds,	19
HYPOCHONDRIAC,	35
HYPOPHOSPHATES,	86
INFANT POWDER,	68
INFLUENCE, of the Mother upon the Offspring,	14
INFANTILE LIFE, How Divided,	120
INHALATION,	64
INORGANIC MATTER,	14
IMPURE AIR, Effects of,	128

INDEX.

	Page.
INSTITUTIONS OF LEARNING, Mixed,	26
KIESTINE,	73
LACING,	52
LANDAU, Siege of,	34
LAW AND ORDER,	10
LAWS OF SEX,	22
LICENTIOUSNESS,	9
LIBEIG'S SOUP,	102
LIFE, Division of,	120
MARRIED PEOPLE,	9
MARRYING EARLY,	27
MARKS, Mother's,	40
MALE, Cultivation of	26
MALE, Duties of,	21
MATERNAL Influence Upon the Offspring,	14
MASCULINE WOMEN,	22
MATERIAL Conditions of Matter,	31
MAMMARY Abscess,	75–94
MEDICINES, How Administered,	120
MILK, White,	74
Yellow,	71
MENTAL Exercises of the Pregnant Female,	41
MIXED Schools,	26
MOTHERS, Changes in During Uterine Gestation,	72
of Great Men,	20
MOUTH of the Infant,	122
Changes in,	125
MUCUS, Discharge of,	
MUSCLES,	81
NERO,	7
NEWLY-BORN, Management of,	58
How Treated by the Romans, Spartans, etc.,	58–59
NEIGHBORS, Advice to,	118
NIPPLES, Contracted,	93
NOISE,	111

INDEX.

	Page.
NURSE, Wet,	103
NURSING the Infant,	69
Posture,	69
NOURISHMENT,	125
NOSTRILS, Closing of,	123
ORGANICAL CONSTRUCTION,	15
ORGANISM, Changes in,	36–38
ORGANIC LAW,	7
Matter, Distinctive Feature of,	13
PAP, Carrot,	102
PARENTS, Duties of,	6–7
PARENTAL CHARACTER, Transmission of,	7
PARENT CELL,	13
PASSION, Effects of, on the Milk,	105
PATERNAL INFLUENCE upon the Offspring,	7
PART I,	5
PART II,	28
PART III,	58
PART IV,	80
PART V,	110
PHYSICIAN,	115
PHYSICAL EXERCISES of the Pregnant Female,	41
PHOSPHATES,	74
PRIMORDIAL CELL,	13
PREPARATION OF FOOD, Care in,	97–100
POST MORTEM, Results of,	66
QUIETUDE,	111
SALIVARY GLANDS,	98
SEX, Distinctions of,	22
Necessity of Complying with the Laws of,	22
What is,	21–22–23–24
SCHOOLS, Mixed,	26
SEIGE of Landau,	34
SENSITIVENESS, Note,	38
SLEEP,	76

	Page.
SMELLING, Sense of,	64
SPERMATOZOA,	14
SPIRIT or Soul,	15
STAYS,	50
STREETS, Corners of,	83
SUGAR,	74
Refinery,	46
TASTE, Sense of,	64
TEETHING,	84
TEMPERATURE,	61–111
TEETHING, Stages of,	86
TOUCH, Sense of,	61
URINE of the Fœtus,	47
VALVE, Foramen Ovale,	66
VENTILATION,	65
VERNIX CASEOSA,	60
VISITORS, How to Receive,	118
WALKING,	52–84
WASTE MATTER in the System,	45
WATER,	90
WATCH, Illustration by,	11
WEANING,	108
WET NURSE,	99–104

PUBLICATIONS OF
PETER G. THOMSON,
179 VINE STREET,

<u>ARCADE BOOKSTORE.</u> CINCINNATI, O.

---o---

CINCINNATI'S BEGINNINGS: Being the Early History of the City and the Miami Purchase, from hitherto Unpublished Documents. By FRANCIS W. MILLER. Large 12mo. - - - - - $1 75

    The most important work yet published relating to the History of Cincinnati; it gives the early events in the settlement in the words of the settlers themselves, and explodes many of the old theories that have hitherto been looked upon as facts.

SIXTEEN SAVIOURS OR ONE? The Gospels not Brahmanic. By JOHN T. PERRY, of the Cincinnati Gazette. 12mo. Paper, 50 cents. Cloth, - - - - . - - - - - 75 cents.

    "This work of Mr. Perry is one of vast and compressed erudition and victorious criticism, and is destined to be of permanent value. It ought to be in every minister's library, on the table of every lover of truth, in the home of every workingman, and in the hands of all our youth. We do not know of another instance, in our day, where any member upon the editorial staff of the secular press has appeared in so handsome and triumphant a role against the popular and plausible scepticism of the age. It is a book for which Mr. Perry will have the thanks of the whole Christian world."—*Cincinnati Commercial.*

    "The mass of information contained within the limits of this work is simply astonishing. It affords a treasury of reliable data and authorities upon this difficult subject which is invaluable; and, as the price of the book is very low, we trust it will be widely circulated."
                                                      —*Herald and Presbyter.*

Publications of Peter G. Thomson, Cincinnati.

CREED AND GREED. Lectures by the Rev. DUDLEY WARD RHODES, of Cincinnati. 12mo. Cloth extra, - - - - - $1 25

These Lectures have met with a glorious reception, and been reprinted in newspapers throughout the country. The topics are: Food Corruptors; Tradesmen's Books; the Story of the Auditor's Books; Street Car Life in Cincinnati; The Curse of Tenement Houses; The The Betrayal of a City; Church and Theater; Common Sense in Funerals.

" Mr. Rhodes has a remarkably honest, straight-forward, thorough and manly way of examining into the merits of the case at hand, and if there were more of his kind in our pulpits, there would be less of trickery in business, less cruelty in society, less wretchedness and vice everywhere."—*Chicago Advance.*

GUIDE TO THE EXAMINATION OF URINE, with special reference to the Diseases of the Urinary Apparatus. By K. B. HOFFMAN, Professor at the University at Graz, and R. ULTZMANN, Docent at the University of Vienna. From the Second Edition, translated and edited by F. FORCHHEIMER, M. D., Professor of Medical Chemistry at the Medical College of Ohio. WITH ILLUSTRATIONS. 12mo. Cloth, $1 50. Leather, - - . - - - - $2 00

This work is used as a text book in the Cincinnati Medical Colleges, and in many other cities, and is the recognized authority on the subject.

THE HEALTHY INFANT: A Practical Treatise on the Healthy Procreation of the Human Race. By TANDY L. DIX, M. D. 12mo. Cloth, - - . - - - - - - $1 25

A BOOK FOR EVERY HORSE-OWNER. The Horse's Foot and how to Shoe it. Giving the most approved methods of horse-shoeing, together with the Anatomy of the Horse's Foot and its Diseases. By J. R. COLE. WITH FORTY-TWO ILLUSTRATIONS. 8vo. Cloth, $1 00

" This book is sold for less than the price of a single set of shoes, and we can warrant that every farmer or horse-owner who is not already well informed in everything relating to the care of the horse's foot, will find himself well repaid in the investment."—*New England Farmer.*

" The importance of the subject demands the thorough discussion that is given it in this volume. By means of numerous illustrations and plain language, the author makes all the intricacies of the horse's foot clear to the average reader, and enables him to know what is the matter with the foot, when the horse goes lame after shoeing. It shows what few blacksmiths know—how to shoe a horse properly. This information alone is worth the cost of the book to every horse-owner."—*Indiana Farmer.*

Publications of Peter G. Thomson, Cincinnati.

CINCINNATI SOCIETY BLUE BOOK, AND FAMILY DIRECTORY, Containing the names of householders, giving their private residences, and exact numbers, together with the names of the adult members of each family, the ladies' reception days, etc., etc. With a complete classification by streets and suburbs. 12mo. Cloth, elegant, gilt edges. (By Subscription only.) - - - - - $5 00

LOTOS LAND, and other Poems. By G. S. LADSON. 16mo. Cloth, Gilt. - - - - - - - - - - $1 00.

THE LIBRARY CATALOGUE. Ruled and arranged to suit any number of volumes. 4to. Cloth, - - - - - - $1 50

    A great convenience, in fact, a necessity, to every one who owns a library, whether large or small. The book is made of heavy paper, neatly and strongly bound in cloth, with red edges. The following are the printed headings: Title, Shelf or Number, Author, Volumes, Size, Where Published, Date of Publication, Where Bought, Cost, When Bought.

WASHINGTON COUNTY AND THE EARLY SETTLEMENT OF OHIO. By ISRAEL WARD ANDREWS, President of Marietta College. 8vo. Paper, 75 cts. Cloth, - - - - - $1 25

    An epitome of the events connected with the early settlement of Washington County, the first county settled in Ohio, and incidentally of the early History of the State.

MARIETTA COLLEGE in the War of Secession, 1861-65. 8vo. Paper, - - - - - - - - - - 75 cts.

    Contains a history of Marietta College in the War, by President I. W. Andrews, together with biographical sketches of the students who fell in service, and a complete Military Record of the Alumni.

REFERENCES to the Coinage Legislation of the United States. By Col. C. W. MOULTON. 8vo. Paper. - - - - 30 cts.

THE BOOK-BUYER'S GUIDE. A classified catalogue of 170 pages. Sent free to any address.

PETER G. THOMSON,

ARCADE BOOKSTORE,

CINCINNATI.

Library Agency

FOR THE

ECOMOMICAL PURCHASE OF BOOKS.

———o———

The undersigned makes it a special and important part of his business to attend to orders for **Public Institutions** and **Individuals** who desire to have accurate information and suggestions as to the best books and the best editions, and to purchase what they need, whether in thousands, or a single book, in the most economical way.

Orders for American or Foreign Books of every description, whether for whole libraries or single books, are carefully and promptly executed, on the most favorable terms for correspondents. Books, etc., for incorporated institutions, are imported free of duties. Catalogues of the English Antiquarian Booksellers are received regularly, and will be forwarded to any address.

REFERENCES.

State Historical Society of Wisconsin.

The punctuality and intelligence evinced by PETER G. THOMSON in filling the orders, both American and Foreign, for this Library, deserve our recognition and commendation.

LYMAN C. DRAPER, *Secretary.*
DAN'L S. DURRIE, *Librarian.*

Mercantile Library of Baltimore.

The Cincinnati Public Library is to be congratulated in securing you as its agent. I cannot recall anyone who could fill the position with so much credit as yourself. * * My business transactions with you have been of the most satisfactory character. * * What Librarians and Book Committees want, (after plentiful income) is a discreet agent—not a mere picker-up —but one who has knowledge of books and uses that knowledge for the benefit of his principal. I think you completely fill this want.

JNO. W. M. LEE,
Librarian Mercantile Library and Maryland Hist. Society.

Cincinnati Public Library.

American and English books purchased for the Public Library of Cincinnati, are now ordered through PETER G. THOMSON, who has contracted for supplying them on more favorable terms than the Library has ever been able to obtain from any American Bookseller or Importer.

THOMAS VICKERS, *Librarian.*

Chicago Public Library.

I have no doubt but that your long experience in the book business, and your relations with your London correspondent will enable you to serve your customers more satisfactorily than the general book trade can do it. I am also convinced that it is better for libraries and private buyers to use such an agency as yours, rather than import through the regular American booksellers. Wishing you much success in your business, I remain,

Yours very sincerely,
WILLIAM F. POOLE.

All Communications Promptly Answered.

PETER G. THOMSON,

Bookseller, Stationer and Importer,

Arcade Bookstore, 179 Vine St.   CINCINNATI.

www.ingramcontent.com/pod-product-compliance
Lightning Source LLC
Chambersburg PA
CBHW030435190426
43202CB00036B/1282